Flowercraft

Violet Stevenson

Book Club Associates

London

DEDICATION

To Jeremy, because so much of what is here
has been a part of our family life.

ACKNOWLEDGEMENTS

The author would like to give special thanks to her
husband Leslie Johns who has taken most of the
photographs used in this book. She would also like to
thank The British Tourist Authority for the photograph
on p. 143; Bruce Coleman for the photograph on p. 103;
Colour Library International for the photograph on p. 95;
Pix Photos for the photograph on p. 90; Spectrum Colour
Library for the photograph on p. 70, the photograph of
Well Dressing on p. 87 and of the Hallowe'en mask on
p. 102; and Tony Stone Associates for the photograph
on p. 30/31 and on p. 107.

Line artwork by Anne Hutchison

First impression 1977
This edition published 1978 by
Book Club Associates
By arrangement with The Hamlyn Publishing Group Limited
Reprinted 1984
Copyright © The Hamlyn Publishing Group Limited, 1977

Filmset in England by Tradespools Ltd., Frome, Somerset
in 11 on 13 pt. Monophoto Garamond
Printed in Spain

Flowercraft

Contents

Flowers for Scents and Beauty

How pleasing it is that we can capture the fragrance of some flowers, that we can keep some of them in essence as it were. Flowers and fragrant foliage have been gathered wild and cultivated and used fresh or dried in some way or another since the beginning of civilisation. Nothing stirs the remembrance of happy, sunny spring and summer days so much as the scent of potpourri made from plants which were at their zeniths then. And, if I can be forgiven for being quite sentimental, a splash of rose-water on a tired skin in mid-winter can be as refreshing as the sight of a dewy rose on a summer morning.

It is also pleasing, and interesting, to learn that today more and more people are seeking knowledge on how they too can preserve the scent of flowers. Perhaps it is because once one knows the true scents, the synthetic are usually quite unsatisfying – indeed, they can become offensive.

In the following pages are recipes for preserving some of the fragrance of a variety of the most scented flowers, all of which, alas, are too fleeting and often fade before we have had full opportunity to savour them deeply. Potpourris and other scented items help us hold on to the flowers a little longer. All of my recipes are quite simple and I have included only those which I know can be prepared with flowers from the garden, and I have mentioned only those ingredients which I know can be bought, although I must admit that some of these have led me on a search, but even the searches have had their fun and entertainment.

If you have ever visited a museum devoted to the manufacture of flower perfumes, such as exists at Grasse in Provence, you will have formed some idea of the many and involved processes used to extract the essential oils and fragrances. The most highly scented toilet waters and perfumes have at some point been distilled. I feel that few amateurs would wish to go to the expense and trouble which distillation involves; however, should you be curious as to how this is done, in one case, at least, turn to the section on Violets on page 36. Meanwhile, I urge you to make some of the more simple of the flower perfumes be these potpourri, toilet water, cream, salve or even hair rinse.

Certain flowers, such as lavender, are used in potpourri, but they are also featured in their own right, being made into special kinds of scented items such as lavender bottles, sachets, sweet bags, water, vinegars, sugars and other items.

Potpourri

I consider myself to be a very busy woman yet this is always to be found in my home, possibly because it is so easy to make and can be done in odd moments when it is extremely relaxing to handle

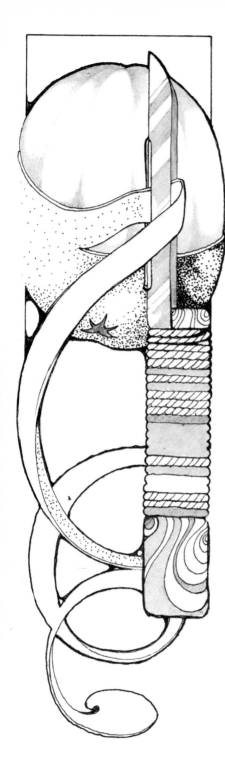

such pleasant things. I like to place a bowl in the guest room and this is always appreciated, especially by visitors from town or city. Nothing seems to give them so much pleasure as a going-away gift of a bag of mature potpourri made from plants from my own garden with a few from the countryside around the cottage.

Packed loosely yet airtight in a plastic bag, such a gift offers no problems, for it will lie flat and take little room in a suitcase as well as being very light. Once home, the contents can be poured into bowls, sewn into sweet bags or pillows where they remain fragrant souvenirs, not only of a pleasant visit, but also of a garden and a little corner of the English countryside made familiar through senses other than that of sight alone.

Scents in history

Before mats, rugs and carpets were laid down in the home and when domestic hygiene came nowhere near today's standards, many floors, especially those of downstairs rooms, were covered with a layer of 'strewing' herbs. Floors were damp and the herbs helped to keep conditions relatively dry underfoot but, equally important, some of the herbs – mostly of the leafy type which gave off a pleasant fresh scent when bruised underfoot – were also considered to be prophylactic and effective in warding off fevers.

Tussie-mussies were posies of scented flowers and leaves which were held in the hand and brought constantly to the nose as one walked abroad in times of epidemic or when one was forced to pass through some unsavoury or plague-ridden neighbourhood. They were also considered to be febrifuges and were stood in water and placed about the home. It seems that the antidote to unpleasant vapours was believed to be sweet, natural fragrances and all highly scented flowers were greatly prized.

Obviously, both the strewing herbs and the posies contained ingredients which dried naturally and which were found to last well and to remain scented, at least to some degree. Since few fresh flowers could be obtained in autumn and winter, it was only to be expected that ways would be found to preserve the flowers and the characteristic fragrances of the best of the herbs and flowers so that they could be available at any time of the year.

This, then, is the basis of potpourri. The French word means a mixture, originally of meat as in a stew, even of songs and, if we take it literally, a rotten pot. Today, it is simply a mixture or a blend of fresh, partly or wholly dried flowers, usually their petals, leaves, seeds or even roots, though entire flowers of some kinds are used. All should be scented or they should be those kinds, like orris or iris root, which become scented after drying and storing, and which will hold that same scent for several months or even, as you will discover, in some cases for years.

Potpourri varies considerably, which adds to its charm, and in

Dried and powdered orange peel makes a good fixative for the fragrance of potpourris.

spite of following a recipe, it is unlikely that one ever makes the same potpourri twice. Indeed, I suggest that all recipes be taken as guides, for I have never found that, by using a little less of one flower and a little more of another, the result is any the less pleasing. It is even possible to make potpourri from just two kinds of flowers or an extremely simple type by collecting scented flower petals and fragrant leaves, drying them and mixing them together. The mixture will be scented, but it will not be very strongly scented or remain scented for very long.

Fixing the fragrance

Fortunately, it is possible to fix the fragrance and to do this one should include one or more fixatives in the mixture. These also vary considerably, but it is reassuring to know that one of the best fixatives, and one which adds a little of its own perfume to a mixture, is citrus peel – tangerine, orange or lemon peels are the best. The peel can be pared finely using an apple parer, dried slowly in a barely warm oven or over a stove (put the parings in a net bag and hang this up in the warm, dry air stream), and then ground to a powder in an electric blender or a coffee grinder.

As an alternative I often use the following method. After squeezing the juice from any of these fruits and while the half skin is still

The powdered roots of the stately *Angelica archangelica* are useful for fixing the fragrance of potpourris.

13

soft, I turn it inside out, pull off all the pith and stand it in a dry warm place, in summer simply on a sunny windowsill indoors. When the skins are completely dry I cut them up and grind them. Incidentally, these half skins are very tough and I find that a quick and easy way to cut them is to use florist scissors.

If you have ever grown or planted angelica, no doubt you will have discovered that its roots are fragrant. The most important fixatives are made from dried roots of a few plants which are then powdered or pounded, see below. Perhaps the best known of these is orris root, an iris species root which is scentless when fresh but gives off a fragrance much like that of violets as it ages. It is possible to buy this, but sources seem to be difficult to find. Some chemists and herbalists stock it as well as those stores which deal in a great variety of imported exotic foods and spices.

Other fixatives made from roots include a palm, calamus, and khus-khus or *Andropogon squarrosus* which is a fragrant grass, also sometimes known as cus-cus, vetiver or vetivert, with a scent which is much akin to sandalwood. Angelica, already mentioned, and Sweet Cicely are two kinds which are easily grown in gardens and which readers might like to prepare for themselves.

Gums, which are plant secretions, are also used and of these gum benzoin and gum storax can be bought in powdered form. Sometimes, 'frankincense' or gum olibanum, really a resin, can be found and this is a good fixative.

The more fixatives which are used in a mixture the longer will its fragrance last.

Many recipes of various potpourri call for alcohol as well as certain essential oils such as oil of bergamot, musk, lavender and others. These are used mainly to establish or fix a certain fragrance; however, as one would expect from substances as volatile as these, the essential scents are soon expended. These oils are becoming more difficult to find and I doubt whether they are worthwhile. Also used in some recipes are so-called balsams but these have nothing to do with the garden flowers of that name. Balsam can be a fragrant mixture of ethereal oil and resin or it can be some specific resin, such as that from toluifera, which is lemony and fragrant. There are several balsams, some being more prized in one country than in another, and these may be available from Indian shops and some chemists.

As I have already mentioned, orris root plays an important role in many recipes. If you wish, and are prepared to take the trouble, this can be substituted or supplemented by roots of angelica, Sweet Cicely, and certain hardy geraniums such as *pratense* and *macrorrhizum*, all of which can be grown in the garden. Incidentally, angelica roots are not fully mature until the plant has flowered. Once this has happened the plant dies and can be lifted. If you want angelica for cooking, grow extra plants and cut off the flower

Opposite The old-fashioned roses, such as these Fantin Latour, look delightfully informal in home decorations. Here they are arranged with sprays of single *Rosa willmottiae* in a candlecup. Some species roses have dainty, even fragrant, foliage. (A few clusters of rose-coloured escallonia add substance and colour to the arrangement.) Although, unlike modern hybrids, the season for these roses is a short one, they are so scented that made into potpourri their perfume lingers on in the home until the next summer's flowers bloom again. Or if you refresh the potpourri, it will last even longer.

buds when these appear; this will cause the stems to grow very thick.

To prepare the roots wash and slice them as finely as possible and dry them slowly in a barely warm oven or in an airing cupboard. When the slices are brittle they can be pounded, ground or minced and the resulting powder stored in airtight jars. If you intend to make several lots of potpourri, it is wise always to have some of this powder in store. Better still, mix some spices so that these also are ready to sprinkle over the leaves and petals when they come to hand. A good basic recipe is as follows: 2 oz (55 g) of any one or mixed powdered root, 1 oz (25 g) cloves, 1 oz (25 g) cinnamon, ½ oz (14 g) each nutmeg, coriander, citrus peel, all powdered.

If the foregoing list seems forbidding, some readers may be relieved to learn that coarse salt, sometimes called bay salt, is also a good – and cheap – fixative. I have found that potpourri made with no spices or fixatives other than powdered citrus skins and salt keeps its fragrance for a long time. This is particularly the case with roses, even if petals fallen from flowers used in arrangements – as opposed to those gathered fresh – are used. An old recipe I have recommends that roses pounded or well rubbed into one fourth their weight of salt (very little really since rose petals are not heavy) and kept in a jar will retain their scent for years. The same writer remarks that rose-water made from water distilled from salted roses is much stronger than that made from the 'fresh blown rose'.

Making 'moist' potpourri

Salt was widely used at one time and, of course, it is a preservative. It was, and is, essential in 'wet' or 'moist' potpourri. These terms are still applied to recipes in which salt is used although the ingredients are quite dry before they are mixed; this causes some confusion, as you can imagine. Truly moist potpourris depend to a great extent on the correct flowers being used; these are, mainly, fresh or just partly dried roses, violets, philadelphus or mock orange, lily-of-the-valley, pinks, carnations, any kinds which do not become mouldy or sour – as do stocks, for instance. I imagine that it was mixtures such as these that were the original 'rotten pot'.

A recipe dated 1890 gives some guidance, and although this is perhaps too involved for modern tastes, it is a gem in its own right. 'Gather the roses on a dry day only, and lay them on sheets of newspaper to dry in the shade, then sprinkle them freely with finely powdered bay-salt. Pound smoothly together a quantity of musk, gum benjamin, dried Seville orange peel, angelica root, cloves, Jamaica pepper, coriander seed, and spirits of wine. Now take sun-dried rose leaves, clove carnations, lavender, woodruff, rosemary, violets, etc., and place them in layers in a china or

earthenware jar, alternately with salt and the pounded spices mentioned above. Or, pound very fine, 1 lb bay-salt, 2 oz. salt-petre, ½ oz each of cloves and allspice, and mix these thoroughly with a grated nutmeg, the very finely pared rind of four lemons (being careful to omit all white pith), 1 dr of musk, 1 oz bergamot, 6 dr powdered orris root, and 1 dr each of spirits of lavender, essence of lemon, and storax. Have ready minced a handful each of bay leaves, rosemary, myrtle, lemon thyme and sweet verbena. Place these all, when well hand-mixed, into a jar with a close fitting lid, adding to them, as you can get them, six handfuls of sweet-smelling and dried rose leaves (these must be petals I imagine, V.S.), three of orange blossom (philadelphus?), three of clove pinks and two each of rosemary flowers, lavender flowers, jasmine flowers and violets. *The roses must be gathered on a perfectly dry day,*

Philadelphus, or mock orange, produces its sweetly scented flowers in summer. As well as being a delightful garden shrub, the flowers make sweet bags or can be used in potpourri.

17

and may then, if liked, be placed in the jar at once – and the same applies to other blossoms, for all sweet-scented flowers (so long as they are not succulent) can be used for potpourri – stirring them all well into the mixture, for potpourri cannot be too much stirred, especially at first. *But remember no flowers must be added while the least damp, either from rain or dew.*' The italics are mine.

The recipe goes on to say, 'If the potpourri appears to become too dry, add more bay-salt and saltpetre; if too moist, add more spice and orris root; but always start your beau-pot (as our grand-mothers called it) with the quantities given above, adding more flowers from time to time, as the spice retains its strength for years.'

The term 'succulent' used above may be a little misleading, for instance, one would say that rose petals are of a succulent nature, but there are some scented flowers which have a much greater moisture content. The most important of these from the pot-pourri maker's point of view are lilies. What a pity it is that we cannot capture their scent this way. Lilies-of-the-valley are not true lilies and these dry and can be used.

Most scented leaves can be used safely in moist potpourri. Spices, such as cinnamon, allspice, cloves and orris root are also used and it is wise to include a little brandy or some other spirit as a preservative. Potpourris of this type should be kept in the special potpourri jars which have perforated lids. These are collectors' pieces now, but perhaps some enterprising potter will begin making them again one day.

Spicing mixtures

Not only flowers but fragrant leaves and seeds can be used in all kinds of mixtures. The seeds are usually ground or pounded to become spices. Some plants produce flowers, leaves, seeds and even stems which are scented and which can be used. Basically, the proportions are a quart (generous litre) of flower parts to a half pint (285 ml) of leaves. There are some extremely pleasant mixtures which can be made from scented leaves alone and these are especially good for placing about the home in bowls. The contents should be stirred from time to time and slightly bruised to release the aromas.

Choosing flowers for potpourri

Each garden is likely to have its own contribution of scented plants to offer, and I would advise those with small gardens who are doubtful if they have enough to gather to go to the cooking herb patch as well as to the flower border because thymes, rosemary, mints, fennel, even sage, can play a part. Where wild flowers abound it should be possible to gather some without endangering the species. Each locality or country will have its own kinds; in

Opposite My own herb garden serves two purposes, for it also divides the caged fruit and vegetable garden from the ornamental section. Mounded, well drained and running east to west, those plants which need sun can be given their full share. High on the mound bronze and green fennel, with southernwood, makes a tall summer screen and provides a dense feathery foil for the hues of lavender, borage, hyssop, costmary, mingled with sages, marjorams and others. Thymes grow over the lower edge. On the cooler, shady side, mints, lemon balm, chervil, tansy and Sweet Cicely flourish.

my own Cotswold area I can find masses of wild marjoram, meadowsweet and hawthorn, to mention but three. Others can be cultivated and most are highly decorative. Some such as lavender and roses can be made into important features of a garden.

Flowers bought from the shop can sometimes be included. For instance, I never throw away freesias. As soon as one of the florets looks a little past its best, I nip it off and put it away to dry. It retains some of its scent and it contributes another colour to the mixture.

Always popular with the bees, the blue borage flowers can be pressed and used to decorate boxes of potpourri.

Appearance is important and I think that it is worth including a few special flowers for colour alone even though they do not produce much perfume. Of these borage and anchusa contribute a beautiful blue, but they should be gathered just before they open if they are to retain their full colour. I like also to press heartsease and any small violas or pansies to scatter on the surface of a mixture, especially when this is packed in a transparent box as a gift.

There are many sweetly scented flowers blooming in the early part of the year including some of the shrubs. These can be used for special spring potpourris (page 23). Alternatively, flowers gathered at this season can be stored and later mixed with summer flowers.

If you would like to try a moist potpourri, may I suggest that you begin in spring with some violets and lily-of-the-valley. From the way these behave, you will be able to judge whether or not you wish to make more moist potpourri later in the year.

It should be borne in mind that there are many flowers in our gardens now which were not cultivated at the times when potpourris were widely made and, therefore, you are not likely to find their names in really old recipes. However, this is not to say that these cannot be used. Dry a small sample quickly (in an oven or over a radiator) so that the flowers or leaves can be tested for scent. Crumble them between the fingers and smell not only them, but your skin as well.

I am constantly trying new mixtures and I am interested to learn just how many flowers respond to this type of preservation. Many of my early experiments were with petals which fell from flowers used in arrangements, or which were plucked from them when the arrangement was dissembled. It seemed to me that if mixtures from these were successful, then they would be even better if the flowers were freshly gathered. This has proved to be the case; even so, I seldom throw away rose petals which have fallen. I have found that, quite often, drying the petals and mixing them with other materials brings out the perfume, even sometimes from a rose which seemed fairly unscented when it was growing.

It is interesting, also, that when fresh ingredients, either of one kind or mixed, are added to old and seemingly tired mixtures, they will rejuvenate them. Strange as it may seem, this will sometimes result in a potpourri which is much more fragrant than it was in the first place.

Having said this, I should stress that if you wish to make really good potpourri it is well worthwhile searching for and planting the most highly scented kinds and varieties. Some varieties of roses, pinks, mock orange and other kinds of flowers are much more scented than others. Sometimes a flower is of no or little value, whereas its foliage will be highly scented. This is the case with some of the scented-leaved pelargoniums.

A Few Personal Recipes

Lemon-scented potpourri

This is a mixture which I like to use for gifts. Apart from the fact that everyone I know appears to enjoy the clean scent of lemon, the potpourri looks attractive, particularly when presented in little storage jars. Have pansies pressed ready, yellow or mainly yellow ones, and place these against the side of the jar so that they are facing outwards. The best way to do this is to put the lowest flower in first and then to hold the jar in such a way that the pansy stays in place. Then pour in enough mixture to secure it. If a pansy is to go on the other side, keep the mixture on one side only until the second flower is in place. Repeat the process as you position more pansies and gradually fill the jar.

Dry plenty of scented spring flowers, such as wallflowers, jonquils or other kinds of narcissus, freesias and azaleas, whatever you have but keeping the main colour yellow. To these add the summer flowers, including yellow roses and, if you can, lime, as these become available. With these flowers go a larger proportion of scented leaves than is usual in potpourri mixtures, 3 cups to 1 of flowers, but if this is not possible add extra lemon peel. Ideally, the leaves should include dried melissa or lemon balm, lemon thyme, variegated pineapple mint, southernwood, lemon verbena or lippia and *Pelargonium crispum*, the lemon-scented geranium. Add ½ teaspoon powdered lemon peel, 1 oz (25 g) orris root and 6 drops lemon verbena oil or citronella.

Right Dried scented leaves of all kinds, fragrant petals or whole tiny flowers, can be used in a potpourri. Fixatives to hold the perfumes are important. They range from exotic gums and root powders to coarse salt and citrus rinds.

A simple spring potpourri

Wallflowers and rosemary bloom at much the same time. It will take an hour or two to gather the rosemary flowers and if there are not quite enough to make the required quantities a few leaves may be added instead. To each half pint (285 ml) of dried wall-flowers and rosemary (1 pint, 570 ml, in all) use 2 oz (55 g) orris root and 1 teaspoon powdered nutmeg. Mix together well.

It may be helpful for me to point out that orris has a similar scent to that of violets and is used in many 'violet' mixtures. Its inclusion in spring potpourris gives them that particular springtime fragrance.

Philadelphus sweet bags

This is the plant which is known as mock orange, but is also some-times incorrectly called syringa – a name which belongs to lilac.

To 1½ pints (850 ml) of dried philadelphus flowers add ½ pint (285 ml) of rose-scented pelargonium leaves and 1 teaspoon powdered angelica root or, failing this, use orris.

Mix these ingredients really well and then place a tablespoonful or so in small, double thickness muslin bags so that the potpourri can be laid among linen. This is a delightfully fragrant mixture.

Above Among some other herbs, rosemary is an excellent hair rinse and conditioner. A rinse is as simple to make as tea.

Below A selection of sweet-scented gifts; a little hop pillow to help induce sleep, two sweet sachets to place among linen – made from my recipes and given to me by friends – lavender and sweet bags to slip onto coat hangers, lavender bottles, and potpourri strewn with pressed flowers and packed in a paper lace-edged plastic food tray.

Bath bags

Many of the potpourri plants can be used to scent bath water and the most convenient way of doing this is to make them up into bags, in much the same way as one prepares *bouquets garnis* from dried herbs. Use the things which have good oils in them such as rosemary, lavender flowers, mock orange, real orange blossom too if you have it, scented mints, southernwood, bay leaves and pine needles. Throw the bags into a hot bath; alternatively, but this is just a little more fuss, put the bag into a jug and pour boiling water on it before emptying the whole contents into the bath.

Hair rinses and conditioners

There are many recipes for hair rinses and conditioners, although not many of these are made from flowers only. Chamomile is greatly recommended for its quality in keeping blonde hair a good colour. Where possible clean rain water should be used.

Chamomile hair rinse

Place 1 tablespoon chamomile flowers in a jug and pour on a half pint (285 ml) of boiling water. Let this steep for five minutes or so, strain and allow to cool before using.

Rosemary for hair

My own personal recommendation for this herb as a hair tonic is that I once knew a very old lady whose blonde hair was only a little grey. She always used rosemary water as a final rinse.

Prepare the rinse in just the same manner as directed above, using fresh leaves, but let these steep for a quarter of an hour or so.

This infusion can also be used as a lotion for the scalp, in which case it should be rubbed in three or four times a week.

Where the hair is in very poor condition a lotion to be used daily can be made from 2 oz (55 g) rosemary leaves, 2 oz (55 g) southernwood, and $\frac{1}{2}$ oz (14 g) of camphor. Mix these in a jug and pour boiling water on them. Strain and bottle after an hour.

Southernwood hair lotion

As with rosemary, southernwood leaves can be infused and the lotion rubbed into the scalp three or four times a week.

Traditional Potpourri Flowers

There are a few traditional flowers used for making potpourri and flower perfumes. These include lavender, roses, violets, elder, and gilly-flowers.

Carnations and pinks

The deep crimson, clove-scented carnation is the 'clove gilly-flower' of old recipes. The flower was once most highly esteemed, not only for its scent but also for its savour. Here we are most concerned with the first. As a general rule this flower can be used in place of roses.

A writer in 1657 tells us that 'the leaves (petals) of the flowers put into a glass of vinegar, and set in the sun for certain dayes, do make a pleasant vinegar and very good to revive one of a swoon, the nostrils and temples being washed therewith.'

Sweet Williams are close relatives of the carnation and can also be used in potpourri. The individual florets should be pulled from their calyces (the green parts behind the flower) before they are put to dry. If you want to make your own mixture using a quantity

The pinks are a favourite garden flower, but not only the old-fashioned varieties need be used. Many of the modern hybrids and varieties are spicily fragrant. They are also, fortunately, very free flowering.

of petals of any of these flowers, bear in mind that bay leaves have a fragrance much akin to that of the gilly-flower, so use powdered bay as well as cloves in the mixture.

I would suggest, also, that if you prepare a potpourri for gifts, you press some of the prettiest tiny pinks and individual Sweet William flowers and use these to strew over the surface of the potpourri when it is packed into boxes or jars.

A carnation sweet pot, a recipe for a moist potpourri

All the recommended ingredients may not be in flower at the same time; they can, however, be added in stages. Always spread salt over each fresh layer of flowers making this deep enough to cover the flowers completely. When the final layer is added, allow the mixture to mature for about six weeks. After this time it can be placed in a potpourri jar or a ceramic pomander.

2 pints (generous litre) carnation and/or pink petals and 1 pint (570 ml) of philadelphus petals form the basis of the mixture. To these are added handfuls of the following: knotted marjoram, lemon thyme, rosemary, myrtle, scented mint and lavender. Bear in mind that some of these, the marjoram for instance, are often most rich in oils when they come into flower, so where possible use the flowering shoots.

Chop or roughly mince the petals and leaves. Mix in the powdered peel of a lemon and tangerine and $\frac{1}{2}$ teaspoon each of powdered bay leaves and cloves. Put this mixture in layers between coarse salt in a jar, making the lowest layer of the petal mixture.

Scented carnation lotion

Gather dry petals from scented carnations or fragrant pinks and loosely fill a 2-lb (1-kg) preserving jar. On to these pour 1 pint (570 ml) of odourless rubbing alcohol. Cover and shake well. Let the mixture stand for three or four weeks but during this time shake it at least once a day. Have ready little bottles and strain the infusion into them. Cork them well. This will make a fragrant lotion to give to a friend who is bedridden or perhaps only temporarily confined.

This same method can be used for most of the scented-leaved plants as well as for roses, violets, jasmine and mock orange.

Elder

Opposite Gilly-flowers, clove-scented carnations and pinks, grown for centuries, are some of the best flowers for potpourri.

The humble elder tree was once much valued, every part of it which grows above ground being of use to man in one way or another. The lacy creamy corymbs of blossom, often so plentiful

that they seem to smother the branches, feature in many old recipes and I find, to my pleasure, that they are still gathered and used by some of my neighbours and friends in the countryside where I live. (Apart from its utility value, I love the plant for its decorative qualities. Blossom branches stripped of much of their foliage so that they do not wilt make beautiful flower arrangements and last well.)

Not only are the flowers good for cooking (see page 44) and wine making, but they are widely recommended as a salve and skin cleanser. The flowers should be gathered when they are newly opened and not spoiled by rain. The most convenient way of drying them is to fashion a wire-netting 'table' by bending a strip all round the edges so that the wire-netting stands high enough for you to be able to insert the short stems through the mesh while the flowers lie flat on it. Place this on a sheet of paper to catch any flowers which may fall during the drying process and dry them in a warm though not hot place. Strip off the stems later and store the blossom in airtight containers.

Elderflower face cream

It is always difficult to give exact quantities for some flower recipes because so much depends upon the size of the individual flowers and this tends to vary a little from season to season. For the recipes given here, I suggest that you gather a bucketful of flowers. Any left over can usually be dried and mixed into pot-pourri or used for some other purpose.

Melt 1 lb (450 g) pure lard in a heavy saucepan but do not allow it to boil. Add the elderflowers, which should have been stripped from their stalks, until it is obvious that the lard will take no more. Simmer gently for an hour. Strain through muslin or a fine sieve. When cool, add a few drops of good perfume. Pour into small pots.

This cream should last well.

This same process can be followed with Vaseline instead of lard in which case an ointment is made. This is good for rough skins, baby rash, even insect bites.

Cold cream

Place 4 oz (110 g) white wax in a basin and stand it in a warm place. When it is soft gradually beat in 8 oz (225 g) almond oil and 4 fl oz (140 ml) elderflower water. You can also make the cold cream with other flower waters, but elderflower is considered good for the skin.

Elderflower water

Take ½ lb (225 g) of elderflowers, stripped roughly from their stalks, and cover them with a pint (570 ml) of boiling water in a

double saucepan or a basin suspended over a large pan of water.

Cover closely and allow to simmer gently for several hours so that all the juices have been extracted from the flowers. Strain through muslin or a fine sieve. Rinse out a bottle with eau de Cologne and pour in the water. Cork it tightly. This water will only keep for about a week unless it is refrigerated.

Elder blossom has many uses, not only fresh in arrangements but also in wines, cooking and cosmetics.

29

Lavender

The reason that lavender scents the air so delightfully in a garden is because the entire surface of the flowers is covered in minute oil glands. The oil secreted is highly volatile and quickly spent, so it follows that the drier the air and the hotter the sun, the more quickly will this oil be lost. For this reason, lavender should always be gathered early in the day, preferably when any dew has dried off the flowers. However, this and rain can be shaken off if the stems are held in small bunches and swished back and forth through the air. After this, dry slowly in an airy atmosphere – either spread

the stems out on newspaper or lay them on sieves, or hang the thin bunches head downwards.

Lavender bottles, see below, should be made from freshly gathered stems because these are pliable.

Lavender potpourri

This is a beautifully pungent mixture, full of summer scents.

To each $\frac{1}{2}$ lb (225 g) of stripped lavender flowers add $\frac{1}{2}$ oz (14 g) dried thyme, flowers as well as leaves if you can, $\frac{1}{2}$ oz (14 g) scented mint leaves, 1 oz (25 g) coarse salt, $\frac{1}{4}$ oz (7 g) powdered cloves and $\frac{1}{4}$ oz (7 g) powdered caraway seed.

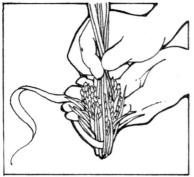

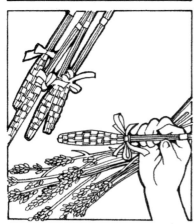

Making lavender scent bottles.

Lavender scent bottles

Once you have made one of these, you will find the process very easy. Take eleven, or a greater odd number, long stems of lavender and about a yard of ribbon. Bunch the flowers, heads level, and tie them together directly under the heads using the ribbon. Holding the bunch in one hand, gently bend each stem, just below the tie, so that it lies on its flower's head. When all the stems are bent over in this way the flowers will be inside a cage of stems. Take the free length of ribbon and weave it through the stems, taking one up and passing the ribbon over the adjacent one. The next time round, take up the stem that was held down last time; it is a little like darning and you will end up with a woven effect.

When you reach the end of the ribbon, or when you have covered as much of the 'bottle' as you wish, stitch the ribbon end in place. Cover this with a little bow. Fix a small strip of ribbon lower down the stems to hold them in place after you have trimmed and shortened the ends to make them all level.

Lavender bags

Be wise, use a little auto-suggestion and select pretty lavender-coloured or lavender-sprigged materials and ribbons for these if you are going to give them away. Somehow even the colour adds to the scent.

To make lavender bags, simply strip the flowers from their stems and, when they are dry enough, pour them into the bags. To conserve every atom of perfume, consider stripping the flowers onto a piece of the fabric, rather than onto paper. If the flowers are ready before the bags, store them in airtight containers.

Apart from laying the bags among linen, it is a good idea to make sack-like bags, gathered and tied at the mouth, for hanging on coat hangers.

Lavender water

Using flowers or leaves, boil a handful in as much water as will just cover them. I prefer to use rain water but this is not essential. Strain the liquid and add to it a teaspoon of brandy to act as a preservative. Pour into a bottle or a scent bottle and cover or cork tightly. Pour the lavender water into bath or washing water as required.

This same method can be used to make scented water of any of the fragrant-leaved herbs, including bay, which, incidentally, is often appreciated by the gentlemen.

Lavender bosses or favours

Use the smallest of the modern foamed plastic globes (see Christmas decorations, page 108) to make a pretty lavender boss with an old-world charm. You need several heads of lavender on short stems, a quantity of lavender shoots, unflowered, a little shorter than the flower heads, and some ribbon.

First thread a narrow ribbon right through the globe so that it can be suspended. This can be done with a bodkin. Loop the lower end so that the ribbon cannot be pulled right through when the boss is hung up. Cover the surface of the globe with the foliage and then the flowers. If you want to make it look more colourful make little loop bunches of lavender-coloured ribbon, tie these to lavender stem ends and push these into the globe.

Roses

A simple potpourri

1 quart (generous litre) dried rose petals, $\frac{1}{2}$ pint (285 ml) dried leaves and/or flowers of marjoram, lemon thyme (or lemon verbena), rosemary and lavender, 1 heaped teaspoon citrus peel, 6 bay leaves, $\frac{1}{2}$ oz (14 g) cloves, 1 teaspoon allspice, these four all powdered, 2 oz (55 g) coarse salt.

Mix the flowers, leaves and spices. Place them in a jar in layers with a sprinkling of salt between each layer. Cover the jar tightly and allow the mixture to mature for one month. After this time it can be placed in jars or in sachets.

Rose and vanilla potpourri

2 vanilla pods, $2\frac{1}{2}$ to 3 pints (1·5 to 1·75 litres) dried rose petals, 2 oz (55 g) orris root, 1 oz (25 g) sandalwood powder (I have substituted ground nutmeg for this with pleasant results), 1 teaspoon powdered cinnamon, 2 oz (55 g) coarse salt.

Mix the spices together. Stand the vanilla pods upright inside each side of the storage jar so that their perfume is given off at the entire depth of the jar. Place the rose petals in roughly 2-in (5-cm) layers. Sprinkle a little of the spice over each layer and cover the layer with salt. Finish with the salt. Cover the jar tightly and store for one month before using it. The vanilla pods can be re-used.

Rose vinegar

At one time, rose and other flower waters and vinegars were to be found on the washstands of most well-organised homes. They offered guests and members of the household a simple means of scenting their washing water or of refreshing foreheads and wrists on hot, dusty days. Unfortunately, fresh rose-water does not last long so it was natural that liquids of a preservative nature were used instead. Rose vinegar is still worth making and it is an acceptable gift for someone who is bedridden. A little poured on a tissue and used as a cleansing pad is extremely refreshing and the perfume has no comparison with that of the manufactured pads.

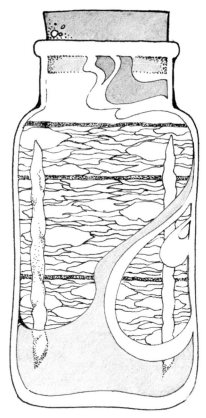

Rose and vanilla potpourri.

New summer scents captive in old
bottles. Fragrant waters make
delightful gifts. In a guest room they
offer an unexpected yet welcome means
for a weary visitor to refresh her face
and hands.

Take a preserving jar, fill it halfway with rose petals and top it
up with white wine vinegar. Cover it and stand it in the sun – a
windowsill is a good place for this – until it has received roughly 24
hours of sunshine. This is following the old recipe, but I do not
think that anything amiss will happen if you run over this time a
little. Strain the liquid off into small bottles.

Rose vinegar will keep indefinitely and, naturally, the more
scented the petals the more perfumed the vinegar.

Rose linen bags

To each pint (570 ml) of dried rose petals, add 1 oz (25 g) powdered
cloves, and 1 oz (25 g) powdered mace. Mix them well. Make little
pillow-shaped muslin bags, using a double thickness of material so
that you do not easily lose the powdered spices, and fill each one
lightly with the petal mixture. Stitch the end. Lay these among the
linen in cupboards or drawers.

A box of these makes a charming present and for this purpose it
is worthwhile making the bags a little more decorative. A rose
decoration seems an obvious choice and a quick and effective way
of doing this is to cut out a rose from a pattern fabric and to
appliqué it to the outer surface of the bag. Alternatively, use an
inner bag of muslin and a rose-patterned fabric for the outer bag.

A rose sleep pillow – a present for insomniacs

For this you will need dried rose petals, powdered cloves and powdered mint leaves. The best mint for the purpose is the sweet-scented variegated pineapple mint; any other mint will do but this has the most delicate scent.

To each pint (570 ml) of petals add 1 oz (25 g) cloves and 2 table-spoons mint. Mix together well. Make a small pillow case of muslin to take the mixture and place this inside a more decorative one. During the day keep the pillow inside a plastic bag so that the scent is not dissipated.

A Rosary

A rosary was originally the name given to a string of 165 prayer beads made from rose petals. These beads are unusual and attractive and can be fashioned into bracelets as well as necklaces and bead collars. They can be made into different sizes if required.

Use pink or red rose petals. Either mince these or chop them finely and cover them with water. They must then be simmered, not boiled, and the process is a lengthy one. The best method is to warm the mixture each day until it is almost boiling and to continue in this way until a little of the resulting pulp can easily be rolled between finger and thumb. The petals become very dark in colour and will turn jet black if they are cooked in a rusty pan. Alternatively, add a few rusty nails to the mixture and remove them later.

When the mass is cool enough, press pieces of it into the size and shape you want. Press hard so that the beads are really solid. Have by you a length of very thick thread or fine twine on a bodkin and, as you make each bead, thread it on to this. Keep moving the beads up and down the thread so that they do not stick to it. Hang the strings in a warm place to dry and move the beads frequently because the holes shrink as they dry.

The finished beads give off a pleasant fragrance when handled. You can, if you wish, scent them in much the same way as a pomander by rolling them in a spice mixture. This will combine with the rose scent; indeed, it will help to fix it.

It is possible to make a pattern on the soft beads by pressing a head of a clove into them – a head incidentally with the flower petals part removed – or by other means, so you might like to experiment.

When the beads are quite dry they can be given a lustre by being rolled round and round in a soft cloth smeared with a little Vaseline. On the other hand, the beads look attractive with a matt finish and after a time they take on an attractive patina.

Attractive and unusual beads can be made from rose petals.

Violets

As one would expect, I have a special interest in these delightfully fragrant little flowers, since the violet is my mother's and my own namesake. I love them, too, and they are among my favourite flowers, most of all the little native species. I was particularly fortunate in growing up in the country and at a time when wild flowers abounded, at a time when one could truly say, 'Who goes a-mothering, gathers violets in the lane.' I am even more fortunate in the fact that wild self-sown violets crop up in many places in my garden. The so-fragrant white as well as the violet cover large areas of the borders or nestle in the grass at the foot of trees, while a little way down the lane that leads to the cottage there is a colony of the purple-red variety, from which I hope one day to steal a runner or two.

The fragrant violet is one of my favourite flowers, useful in potpourris and cooking as well as being delightful, as shown here, in small spring flower arrangements.

First tied in the hand so that they can be stood in the narrow aperture of a crystal ink-well, violets, forced lily-of-the-valley and primroses are framed by variegated ivy leaves.

There are many varieties of cultivated violets, prized mostly for their perfume, both single and double and in various hues. One book on violets which I have lists 108 named varieties but some of these now seem to have disappeared. I urge you to beg a plant of any fragrant garden violet you find growing in an old garden, you may be saving it from extinction. Flowers of the cultivated varieties are usually larger and they have longer and stronger stems, which makes them more acceptable for flower arrangements.

Once they were highly regarded among the 'domesticall' flowers. Violets were used with style in some kitchens and I have more to say about these later. Gerard tells us that 'there bee made of them Garlands for the head, Nosegaies and posies which are delightful to look on and pleasant to smell to'.

These are delightful flowers for a potpourri although I cannot urge you to gather masses of the wild flowers, since I feel that we should leave those for all who pass by to enjoy; on the other hand, if you live where there are a lot, you can hold on to their perfume by preserving them in some way. When you dry and use them, bear in mind that orris root has a similar fragrance to that of violets, indeed it is used instead of them in some sweet bags and scented preparations.

Violets distilled

(The following is taken from *Violets for Garden and Market* by Grace L. Zambra, published by Collingridge.)

A Curious Water known by the name of Spring Nosegay
Take six ounces of violets, a quarter of a pound of hyacinths, the same quantity of wallflowers picked, and jonquils; an ounce of Florentine orris bruised, half an ounce of mace grossly powdered, and two ounces of quintessence of orange. Put the whole, the jonquils, wallflowers and the lilies of the valley (? omitted from the list of ingredients in the book) excepted, about the end of March into a glass body with a gallon of strong spirit of wine; bruise the hyacinths, violets, orris and mace, and towards the end of April add the jonquils when in their highest perfection, that is to say, full blown. A few days after, put in the wallflowers, the petals only, then all the lilies of the valley, carefully picked, and shake all the ingredients well. Eight days after having put in the last flower, empty the infusion into an alembic lute on the head and receiver, which must be placed in cold water, and distil in a cold water bath with a gentle fire.

From the above quantity, three parts of excellent spirit may be drawn off that justly deserves the appellation of the Spring Nosegay.

Grace Zambra adds, 'This recipe has been used by ourselves with great success, and has been marketed by us under the name Windward Spring Flowers'.

A Pomander or Spice Ball

Actually, the word pomander describes a perforated ball of gold, silver or ceramic filled with dried herbs and aromatic spices. At one time pomanders, like tussie-mussies and posies, were carried to ward off infections. Nowadays these pomanders are more likely to be treasured as antiques and the kind with which we are familiar is made from an orange. This type has been with us for centuries and was probably the everyday version of the more valuable kinds. Although orange pomanders are no longer used for their original

purpose, being prized only for their scent, they still are acceptable gifts – if you can bear to part with them once you have made them.

Pomanders can be hung in wardrobes, placed among linen or simply stood or hung in a room where they will give off a sweet, wholesome scent. Once made, their perfume is long lasting, although, as you would expect it remains stronger for a longer period where the pomander is contained inside some cover, even if this is no more than a cupboard or a drawer.

Seville oranges are said to be the best for pomanders but since these are not available at all times of the year or in every place the ordinary kind may be used. Select ripe, thick-skinned fruits. Obviously, the larger these are the more cloves will be needed to cover them, but as a general rule, a medium-sized orange will take an ounce (25 g) of cloves. Also required are powdered cinnamon and orris root, about a teaspoon of these mixed in equal parts to each orange, narrow tape and slightly narrower ribbon, a few pins and a cocktail stick or thin knitting needle.

The tape is used to divide the orange into four equal sections. Pin one end to the top of the fruit and pass the tape right round in one direction, pin it in place and then pass it round in the opposite direction so that the tapes cross. These tapes become discoloured by the oils and juices from the fruit and they should be removed later, after the cloved orange has dried or is almost dry.

Sort the cloves and remove any which are damaged. It is possible to press each clove stem into the orange skin, but this sometimes damages the little buds and it is also tiring. The easiest way is first to pierce the skin with the cocktail stick or needle. Insert one clove at a time and follow the tape edges so that the cloves are set neatly and evenly. Work towards the middle of each section.

When the orange is entirely covered, except for the taped portions, it has to be rolled in the spice mixture. The best way to do this is to put the powder in a bag, lower the orange in and gently shake it or roll it around until you can see that it is completely dusted. Either leave it in the bag (keep the top open if this is plastic to prevent condensation) or wrap the orange lightly in tissue and stow it away in the airing cupboard or in some other dark but dry place for two or three weeks or until the skin under the tape is dry. In any case, remove the tape after two weeks or so in order that the skin beneath can thoroughly dry out.

When dry the pomanders are ready to be decorated. Ends of ribbon should be left so that the pomander can be suspended. Leave an end free to begin with and pin the ribbon firmly in place at the top of the pomander. Take the rest of the ribbon round without cutting it, as you would wrap string crosswise round a parcel. Tie it at the top and pin through the knot so that the ribbon is well secured. The pin will rust and so hold the ribbon fast when the pomander is suspended. Hide this area with a little bow.

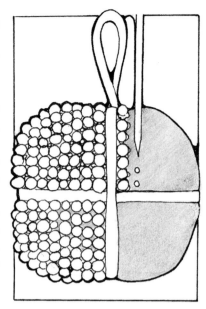

Above Long-keeping apples also can be used. These will shrink more, but pack the cloves closely all the same.

Below Orange pomanders last for years. The cloves not only perfume but also preserve the fruit. After they have been studded with cloves the pomanders are rolled in spices.

39

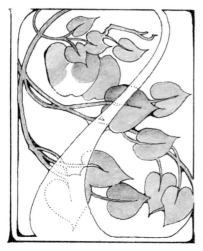

Flowers for Food

The few familiar flowers to be found in our food shops and gardens, the handsome, sculpted globe artichoke – an outsize thistle – the coral-like cauliflower and the pleasing deep purple sturdy shoots or broccoli, are handsome enough for people to use from time to time as decorations and components of special flower arrangements. But how often is it observed that these *are* flower buds which would have come into bloom if they had been left on the plant? We have labelled them vegetables and there they rest. The same can be said of cabbage, Brussels sprouts and many other hearting crops – left too long in the ground they produce a mass of flowers, which we throw away. And those two pungent spices or condiments, cloves and capers, hold the secret of their identity so closely that some people who use them frequently do so unaware that they are cooking with flowers.

The cascading spiny caper plants festoon the old walls of many Mediterranean towns. They are covered with open white flowers with red-tinged petals which are made more beautiful by their striking centres of quivering purple filaments. It is their buds which are pickled and used in sauces. Cloves are buds of the scented little yellow flowers of *Eugenia aromatica*, a plant belonging to the also-fragrant myrtle family. It is a native of the islands of Moluccas and is now grown in many tropical areas.

To study the relationship between flowers and food is to dis-

cover that there are many more waiting to be used, some of them close at hand. These can play a different role from those mentioned above for they will bring interest to many everyday dishes and, more than that, they will also add colour, both exciting and appetising. You will find, for instance, that a fruit cup looks even more inviting if among the mint sprigs and fruit and cucumber slices you stand or float the vivid blue flowers of borage (whose leaves are also cucumber flavoured, so you could dispense with the bought vegetable if you wished).

An ordinary green salad can be given a special cachet if it is garnished with yellow, red and orange nasturtium buds whose taste is as cressy as you could wish. When the plant was first introduced into this country it was known as Indian Cress because of its flavour. It has even borrowed another plant's name, the watercress, which is the true, botanical nasturtium, this again because of its taste, yet most of us grow this attractive and obliging little plant for its decorative value and not for food.

As we walk among the colourful and familiar plants in our modern gardens, it is hard to realise that it was centuries before flowers were cultivated for their beauty alone. At one time, before they were granted growing space, plants had to have gained a reputation, among other things, as prophylactics, curers, healers, restoratives, insecticides or repellents, as wholesome ingredients for food and drink as well as for poisons, as cosmetics and scents.

Herbalists went into the countryside to forage for those kinds which were prized for their particular 'vertues' and, of course, not all had spectacular or pretty blooms, but there were many that had. It was only natural that after a time some of those valued

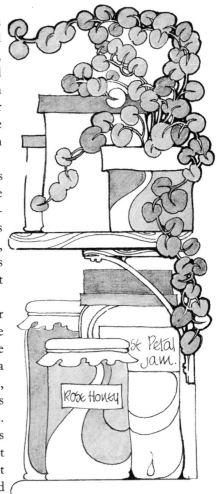

Everyone loves roses and the fragrant old-fashioned kinds are particularly endearing. An informal mass of them for a summer buffet is certain to invite comment and compliments. It will also add to the enjoyment of the occasion, especially when you can describe, or even demonstrate, by some dish on your menu, that they are as wholesome as they are beautiful.

plants would have been cultivated and that as time went by a little corner would always be found for those which had become dear through familiarity, those which revived and refreshed the spirit in ways other than through medicine. Some of our most loved 'cottage garden' flowers are varieties of native species, or even the species themselves, which were originally brought in from the wild so that they would be near at hand and could be cropped more conveniently and also increased.

Furthermore, as the centuries passed many seeds, fruits, roots and sometimes the plants themselves, from those kinds which had proved their worth in other countries, were brought home by travellers. A new flower was often such a fascinating introduction that it drew visitors from miles around to view it, but not necessarily to admire it for its beauty alone.

There was no sentimentality about flowers. Even the lovely rose was originally a utility plant which provided perfumed toilet water, scented lozenges, health-giving salads made from its petals or 'leaves' as these were called, candied petals for sweetmeats and escape from winter scurvy through syrups and soups made from its vitamin-rich hips.

Violets are 'fleurs pectoral', which means that they were used to make a soothing tisane or tea to be taken by those with chest

troubles, and said to be particularly soothing for anyone suffering from whooping cough and asthma. From these same flowers were made much the same things as those which featured roses such as lozenges, sugars, candied flowers, as well as sweet-smelling posies. Many flowers were used for teas and, as far as I can tell, in some cases this was their only use. These teas are still appreciated by many people today and I have given recipes using a number of different flowers on pages 56 to 61.

Although their blooms are not significant, the scented-leaved geraniums (really pelargoniums) are true potted flavour and scent for windowsill gardeners. There are many species, none of which flower handsomely, although I would like to point out that many of the frail-looking blooms press well, but the scent of their foliage makes up for their lack of colour.

The favourite seems to be the rose scented, sometimes simply called the rose geranium. The large-leaved rose is *Pelargonium graveolens* and the little-leaved, *P. graveolens minor*. When you bake a plain sponge cake, lay a star of these leaves on the base of the sponge tin before pouring in the batter. They will give a delicious flavour to the cake. The leaves can also be used to flavour all kinds of desserts, jellies, sorbets, custards, milk puddings and ice-creams.

43

Flowers for Desserts

It seems to me that the flowers often created some interest and variety in a dull diet; for instance, many are recommended for fritters, in French *Beignets de fleurs*. Fritters are easy to make and filling and where there was always lard from a pig and a fire to heat the pan, easy to cook. So we read of borage, rose, violet, marigold, elderflower and other fritters, served with lemon and orange slices. Simple enough and wholesome and still good enough to make today.

Beignets de fleurs

First, make a light batter mixture. Small flowers can be included whole with just the stems nipped off, but use the petals only of larger flowers such as roses. Steep the flowers for half an hour in a little rum or brandy to improve the flavour. (This stage can be omitted if you wish.) Drain and then stir or dip the flowers and petals, according to size, into the batter and deep fry. Drain well on kitchen paper. Serve with sugar and with the spirit in which the flowers were soaked, pouring a few drops on each fritter before it is sugared.

Savoury fritters can be made in much the same manner except that they are not soaked beforehand. Use nasturtium and rosemary flowers, clary and borage leaves, chopped herbs and the male flowers of squash, pumpkins, courgettes, and marrows. If it is necessary to wash the flowers or leaves, drain them well before dipping them into the batter. Serve with lemon juice, or in the case of herb fritters with mint sauce.

Elderflowers are treated just a little differently from the rest because of their shape. Take the entire flower corymb and dip it, face downwards, in the batter. Let the surplus flow off and dry the flower. Leave enough stem to hold the flowers by or it will be difficult to dip them.

Fromage Bavarois aux roses

There is a delicious French sweet called *Fromage Bavarois aux roses* and a simpler American version of this which uses violets as well as roses. I suggest that you also try strongly scented carnations or pinks as well.

You need 1 oz (25 g) of flowers or petals to 1 pint (570 ml) of water and 1 lb (450 g) of sugar. Pick off the stalks and green calyces, wash the flowers and drain them on kitchen paper. Put the water and sugar in a preserving pan and add the flowers – incidentally all one kind, not mixed – stir gently and bring to the boil. Simmer for 20 minutes. Strain and allow to cool slightly.

Measure and allow 1 oz (25 g) of powdered gelatine to each pint

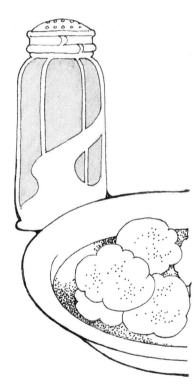

For a sweet with a difference I recommend flower fritters.

44

of syrup. Mix the gelatine with a tablespoon of cold water and add it to the warm mixture. Stir until it is quite dissolved. Use food colouring if you wish; alternatively, colour some of the sugar first by pounding flower petals in it as described on page 48.

When cool, whip the mixture and then add whipped cream at the rate of $\frac{1}{2}$ pint (285 ml) of cream to 1 pint (570 m) of mixture. Pour into a mould or into individual glasses or dishes and garnish with crystallised flowers.

Violet sorbet

> Violets
> 2 teaspoons powdered gelatine
> 1$\frac{1}{2}$ pints (850 ml) water
> 6 oz (170 g) sugar
> Juice of three lemons
> 2 egg whites and a pinch of salt

First prepare the lemon juice. To do this, remove the stems from the flowers and put them with the juice into a basin. You need about a tablespoon of flowers, the more or less you use the deeper or lighter will be the hue of the liquid. Cover the basin and allow the flowers to steep for about 48 hours.

Soak the gelatine in a little of the water, about 4 tablespoons is usually sufficient. Boil the rest of the water with the sugar for 10 minutes. Dissolve the gelatine in the hot syrup and let this cool, and then add the strained lemon juice. Place the mixture in the freezer or in the freezing compartment of a refrigerator and leave until it begins to stiffen. Remove and whisk until it becomes fluffy. Beat the egg whites stiffly and fold them into the fluffy mixture until they are well blended. Return to the freezer and leave for three or four hours. Serve by shaving off layers of the sorbet with a large spoon. Heap into individual dishes and garnish with candied violets.

Pot marigold or calendula

We have neglected this flower during the last century or two. The further I go back in time looking for recipes and evidence of the use of flowers, the more I find about pot marigold. So much so that I have begun experimenting with the petals in various dishes and find them sweet and delicious. They give a good appetising colour to a dish – my marigold custards invite tasting.

The petals can be used in sweets or savouries. They flavour broths, soups and casseroles. In buns, they give the gold of more expensive saffron as well as imparting a very delicate flavour. For an unusual sponge cake, line the base of the tins with marigold petals.

The flavour in this case can be further enhanced if the butter cream filling is flavoured with marigold petals which have been pounded with a little sugar. If the cake is for a special occasion it can be decorated with a flower or two.

It is difficult to give concise quantities because so much depends upon personal tastes. I suggest that you begin with a little and then gradually adjust the recipe so that it is more to your liking.

Apple marigold

This is an unusual and cheap pudding with a particular appeal to those who do not like very sweet dishes.

> 3 large cooking apples
> 2 eggs
> ½ pint (285 ml) milk
> 1 heaped tablespoon sugar or a level tablespoon of honey
> 1 heaped teaspoon of dried marigold petals – more if fresh
> 1 teaspoon lemon thyme, fresh and chopped
> 1 teaspoon sage, fresh and chopped
> Pinch black pepper
> Butter

Peel, core and cut the apples into rings. Beat eggs, milk and sugar or honey together and add the chopped marigolds, herbs and pepper. Pour into a shallow oven dish or a pre-cooked pastry case. Arrange the apple rings on this layer. Dot the butter over the surface and bake in a hot oven for 20 to 25 minutes.

Pot marigold custards

Petals from 12 marigolds (these proportions can be increased to use equal quantities (1 pint, 570 ml) of petals and milk).

> 1 dessertspoon sugar
> 2 eggs
> 1 pint (570 ml) milk
> 6 ramekins or small oven dishes

Pound the petals with the sugar until they form an orange coloured pulp. Beat the eggs in the milk. Add this mixture to the pulp and stir all together until well blended. Put the six ramekins in a roasting tin, not quite touching each other, and divide the mixture between them, stirring it from time to time so that it remains well mixed. Pour water into the tin almost up to the rims of the dishes. Bake in a cool oven for an hour.

These custards can be served hot, but I prefer to let them cool in the tin and then to remove them to the refrigerator for at least an hour before serving. The custards will keep well for two or three days this way.

Opposite Baked egg custards flavoured with marigold petals make a delicious and unusual sweet. If dried petals are used, soak them in the milk until they become soft, then pound them.

Flower Sugars

Again for variety's sake, many kinds of flowers were candied or sugared. They were also used because they added colour to a plain dish. One of the things which so interested me when I began cooking with flowers was the amount of colour just a few blooms could provide. Twelve large violets and a tablespoon of sugar pounded together gave me an attractive pale violet powdered candy, but more than that, changed my attitude about cooking with flowers by adding another dimension. Many flowers were treated in this manner. For instance, few of us today associated lavender with food, yet lavender sugar was once greatly valued. This was made in just the same way as I have made the violet sugar, simply by pounding lavender flowers with three times their own weight of sugar – although I use bulk not weight as a guide. When made, lavender conserve would keep for a year.

Exactly how these sugars were served or used is difficult to discover with certainty, but since we know something of the type of dishes which were eaten, I suggest that they would be sprinkled over some fairly flavourless dish such as plain fritters or boiled suet pudding, junkets and cream.

Today, and for my own use, I find that I get most value from the flowers by applying them to modern dishes. For instance, the violet sugar can be sprinkled over ice-cream just before it is served. It looks well sprinkled in a band round a chocolate cake, or in a floral pattern in the centre.

Vanilla sugar

Vanilla pods are the long seedpods of a climbing orchid *Vanilla fragrans*. Although vanilla essence is now produced synthetically, many cooks prefer to use the natural product.

Keep castor sugar in a jar with one or two vanilla pods and use this for cakes and desserts of all kinds. Be sure to use it when making desserts from flower recipes because the sweet scent of vanilla enhances the flower fragrance.

If you are making vanilla ice-cream, prepare some special vanilla sugar. Use half a vanilla pod to one cup (American measure) of sugar. First cut the pod into small pieces so that it will blend quickly and easily and put it with the sugar into a blender. Turn the machine to high speed and operate it until the vanilla is reduced to tiny black flecks. This sugar can also be used to sweeten whipped cream and this is particularly delicious on hot chocolate or coffee.

Candied Flowers

There is more than one way to candy flowers. Some methods are time-consuming and involve boiling the flowers in the syrup several times. The simplest method (see below) is to paint the petals or flowers and then to dry them well after powdering them with sugar. Petals or flowers should be quite dry before they are candied and I believe that they candy best when they have become a little dehydrated. I suggest that you try a few petals to begin with and then adjust the method to suit yourself. I have dried rose petals completely and then candied them and this type store well.

For one type of coating, beat the white of an egg with a pinch of salt and half a teaspoon of water until quite stiff. The petals should be dipped in this – or painted with the foam – and then covered with sugar until they are heavily coated. I find it best to have by me a shallow bowl or dish containing a shallow layer of sugar. Use a fork or tweezers, lift the petal from the egg white and dip it into the sugar, turning it round until it is completely covered.

Jasmine flowers can be candied, used to flavour sugar and to make tea. They also make a jelly sweetmeat. You need equal weights of flowers and sugar and their combined weights of apple jelly, lemon juice to the proportion of a half lemon to $\frac{1}{2}$ lb (225 g) of sugar. Pound flowers, add lemon juice. Boil sugar to ball stage. Remove pan from heat, add jasmine and juice, stir in jelly. Beat well. Pour into individual sweet shapes or into a tin to be divided later. Dust with sugar. Dry slowly in a cool oven as for meringues. When dry turn out, cut into shapes if necessary, dust again with sugar. Spread shapes on baking sheets and allow to become quite dry in a warm, dry place. Turn occasionally. Place into individual sweet papers. Store between sheets of paper in airtight containers.

Place each sugared petal on greaseproof or wax paper to dry thoroughly. They can be hurried by drying them in a slightly warm oven. These can be eaten or used right away, or they can be stored. Lay them, well spread out, between sheets of paper in an airtight container.

Petals can also be first coated with a syrup containing gum arabic and then dusted with sugar as described above. Gum arabic, which can be bought at chemists or herb shops and some grocers, is a secretion taken from various species of acacia. It is used mainly in confectionery for such chewy sweets as jujubes, marshmallows and liquorice.

To make a small quantity of syrup, crush the gum and soak it in equal parts by bulk of water for 24 hours. Make a thick syrup from $\frac{1}{2}$ lb (225 g) of sugar and 1 pint (570 ml) of water boiled until it reaches 220°F (110°C). Let it cool a little, add the gum solution and bring this to the boil. Skim, strain and bottle or use when cool. It will keep well.

A short cut to candying and a way of making a quick, pretty and wholesome cake decoration is to lightly sugar any of the edible

Above Rose sweets. Pound 1 pint (600 ml) scented petals. Use more if the fragrance does not seem strong enough. Add a teaspoon lemon juice. Beat egg white until it stands in peaks when tested. Add it to 1 lb (450 g) of sifted icing sugar. Beat until smooth. Add the roses and blend well. Turn out paste onto a paper well dusted with icing sugar. Roll out thinly and cut into shapes. Allow to dry before storing.

Right Separate crystallised rose petals are regrouped, largest ones on the outside, to make three roses as a spray for a pink, rose-flavoured iced Valentine cake. Sepals and stems are of angelica. Fern is pressed maidenhair.

daisies such as pot marigolds and chamomile and also some mint leaves. Lightly brush the tips of the ray petals and the surface of the mint leaves with some form of coating and dust the sugar on them. Let them dry a little and make a ring of them round the cake, or arrange a spray in the centre. Use angelica for stems if these are to be featured and sugared mint leaves. A few borage flowers in such a garland adds greatly to its appeal.

A decoration such as this can be made almost at the last moment. Gather the flowers in advance and, if they are dusty, rinse them under water. Stand them in deep lukewarm water so that they become turgid and take off the heads when you are ready to use them.

Any petals you have candied individually can, of course, be reassembled into 'flowers' and these need not necessarily resemble the true flower. However, I have found it possible to reconstruct violets quite easily. Roses and daisies are simple also. So much depends upon establishing a good centre, even if this is only a scrap of angelica, and then arranging the petals around this in as natural a manner as possible.

Above The paste resulting from pounding violets with sugar has many uses. One of the most delicious is in a layer cake. Simply blend the fragrant sugar with your favourite cream filling. Make a pattern of the sugar on the surface also. Store the mixture in jars away from the light.

Left My mother's name is Violet. We need so many candles for each year of her long life that for the past three I have decorated her cake with her name flowers instead. Each violet is made from five individual candied petals grouped around a speck of angelica. The stems and leaves are cut from this candied stem also. It is first soaked in warm water to make it bend.

Roses for Conserves

The best roses for cooking, and this includes conserves as well as candied flowers, are the red varieties, scented, of course. They should be gathered while they are at the peak of condition, fully open but not fading. Inspect the centres, if this is possible, so that you see the firm stamens. Many roses, especially the highly scented old-fashioned varieties have white bases to the petals, sometimes called heels or nails. These have a bitter flavour and should be nipped off. If roses are to be dried and used later for cooking the heels should be removed before drying.

Rose honey

$\frac{1}{2}$ lb (225 g) heeled roses
3 pints (1·75 litres) boiling water
5 lb (2·25 kg) honey

Place the petals in an oven jar and pour the boiling water on them. Stir well and allow the infusion to stand overnight. Strain. Warm the honey in a preserving or heavy pan and add the liquor. Bring it to the boil and let it boil well until it forms a thick syrup. Pour it into warm jars and seal.

Rose syrup

If you hope to make jellies of various flavours and have no apple trees, or perhaps no room for apple trees, one or two rhubarb plants will stand you in good stead. The following recipe explains what I mean.

1 lb (450 g) rhubarb cut into inch slices
1 pint (570 ml) water
$\frac{3}{4}$ lb (340 g) sugar
$\frac{1}{2}$ pint (285 ml) red rose petals, heeled

Simmer the rhubarb until it is pulped and the juice extracted. Strain through a fine sieve. Pour into a heavy pan and add the sugar and the rose petals. Bring to the boil and simmer for 15 minutes. Strain again. Boil the syrup until it thickens and becomes a rich red. Pour into warmed jars and seal.

This can be used as a hot drink and a salve for sore throats. It is also good with milk. In this case, dissolve a teaspoon of the syrup in a tablespoon of boiling water. Allow to cool and add the milk.

Rose petal jam

2 oz (55 g) red, scented, heeled, roses
1 pint (570 ml) water
1 teaspoon lemon juice
1½ lb (675 g) preserving sugar

Boil the sugar and water together until it reaches the candy stage (test by dropping a little in cold water), and then add the lemon juice and the rose petals. Keep stirring the mixture as it boils. When it first comes to the boil add a nut of butter to clear the surface and then simmer for about half an hour, stirring frequently. Test, and when the jam sets, pour it into hot jars. Cover when cold.

Rose-flavoured apple jelly

It is difficult to give exact quantities, but you need apples, sugar, water and dried rose petals. I suggest that you base the quantities on the amount of rose petals you have.

Cut unpeeled and uncored apples into fairly small chunks. Place in a preserving pan and just cover with cold water. Bring them to the boil and then simmer slowly until they form a pulp. Ladle this into a jelly bag and allow the juice to strain through over-night. Alternatively, strain the pulp through a sieve but in this case the jelly will not be as clear as when strained through the bag.

Measure the juice and allow 1 lb (450 g) of sugar to each pint (570 ml). Stir in the sugar until it is dissolved; if the sugar is warmed first on a dish in the oven it will dissolve more quickly. Add a good handful of rose petals, stir, and continue adding them until there are as many as the syrup will hold. Boil for five minutes and test to see if the syrup jels, if it is not quite ready, boil a little longer. Pour through a strainer into hot jars. A jug is the best utensil to use for this purpose.

Apple takes on other flavours well and you can flavour this type of preserve with all kinds of scented flowers and leaves and use them according to their flavours, for instance, mint- and sage-flavoured apple jellies are good served with meat. The same thing applies to baked apples which seem to take the flavour better than stewed apples. Perhaps one has become accustomed to using a clove in apple cooking, but do try other plant flavours. A great favourite with many cooks is the lemon-scented pelargonium leaf, *P. crispum*, with its pretty curled edges. Toss in a little bunch as the jelly is boiling and remove it later.

Flowers for Salads

Colour your salads with flowers and make them more varied and richer in vitamins into the bargain.

One of the prettiest salad plants of all is the showy nasturtium. You can have neat dwarf plants or rampant 'climber' varieties which will so readily cover and hide a bank or piece of poor ground. Nasturtiums are annuals and are easily raised from seed. They will grow in pots or any kind of plant container as well as flourishing on the poorest soil. In fact, they flower best in poor soil.

You can use every part of the plant, leaves, buds, seeds and flowers. If you want a good supply of leaves, sow a few seeds in good soil or feed a few plants rather well.

The bright flowers and half-opened flower buds look as attractive as tomatoes as a garnish. Arrange them on a dish or plate of sandwiches or *hors d'oeuvres* and see how good they look. Try filling the open flowers with a cream or cottage cheese mixed with chopped chives and nasturtium seeds. The latter are good also chopped and mixed in yoghourt as a salad dressing.

The seeds and the flower buds can be pickled and used as capers. Clean and dry them on kitchen paper and pack them into small jars. Mix together 1 pint (570 ml) vinegar, 1 oz (25 g) salt, 6 peppercorns and a bay leaf. Boil and allow to cool before pouring it on the buds or seeds. I think that a fine vinegar, cider or wine, is better than a coarse malt kind. These capers improve with keeping.

Nasturtium sauce

Although this is not strictly a salad it is good with cold meats, cheese and salads. Add a little to a French dressing from time to time to give a different flavour to a salad.

$1\frac{3}{4}$ pints (1 litre) flowers well pressed down
$1\frac{3}{4}$ pints (1 litre) good vinegar
6 to 8 shallots chopped finely
1 clove garlic bruised
1 bay leaf
6 cloves
1 teaspoon salt
$\frac{1}{2}$ teaspoon cayenne pepper

Nasturtium seeds can be pickled and used as capers.

Simmer all the ingredients but the flowers for 10 minutes. Pour the hot liquid on the flowers. Pour all into a large jar and cover it well. Keep it two months and then strain the liquid and bottle.

Rose petal vinegar

Rose petals look and taste good and some people think that a rose petal and green salad suits chicken and turkey best of all. Rose

petal vinegar is easily made and can be used for the dressing to give extra flavour.

Take 3 oz (85 g) of petals to 2 pints (generous litre) of vinegar, preferably a pale vinegar, cider or white wine. Place the petals in a jar and pour the vinegar on them. Cover the jar and stand it in the sun for about a fortnight. If the weather is dull, give it a little longer. Strain and bottle.

Sage jelly is simply apple jelly boiled with a handful of sage, a delicious accompaniment to cold meats or roast pork. Other herbs, mint, rosemary, parsley and tarragon among them, may also be used this way. Scented leaves of pelargoniums flavour jellies for use on breads and desserts.

Herb Flowers

Almost all the herb flowers look and taste good in salads. Inevitably, there will be some that are more to your taste than others, but do try them all. Take chives, for instance. Actually, you should cut the plants so frequently that they do not get a chance to bloom, but you may be like me and prefer to see some plants in flower, especially if they are planted as an edging to a path or border. In this case, allow alternate plants to bloom and cut short the ones between. For a salad, break up the flowers and mix them in – they will give a combined flavour of chives and a taste of honey. Any onion or leek flowers may be used in the same way.

Bergamot flowers are also honey tasting. Hyssop and sage go well in any salad which is served with pork or rosemary with lamb, veal and chicken. The flowers give a less pungent flavour than the leaves.

The very bright blue borage flowers can also be used in savoury salads, but try them as well in a fruit salad or mixture. Candy some of the flowers and use them with angelica and candied mint leaves to decorate any white dish or cream topping, the contrast of blue and green with the white looks so wholesome. Try this on junket, but place the flowers and leaves on the surface very carefully so as not to stir the dish.

Although chervil is grown mostly for its finely cut leaves with their delicate flavour, you will find that once it is allowed to seed itself, there will always be plants in quantity and, since they are to make seed, masses of flowers also. These are white, like smaller versions of the ubiquitous hedge parsley. The umbels are delicate and delightful for use as pressed flowers, but they also make an unusual and delicious soup.

Chervil soup

> 1 pint (570 ml) salted water
> 2 oz (55 g) chervil flowers
> 2 to 2½ oz (55 to 70 g) butter
> 3 tablespoons chopped chervil leaves
> 1 or 2 eggs according to size

Heat the butter with the flowers in it, but do not let it brown or burn. Stir continuously and when it is almost boiling add the liquid in small quantities. Continue stirring. When all the liquid is added, simmer for 10 minutes. Mix in the chervil leaves. Beat the egg or eggs and have ready in a warm but not too hot tureen. Pour in the mixture and serve.

Herb teas or tisanes

These are refreshing, soothing and cheap and most of them can be drunk piping hot or ice cold. All are good with lemon and with sugar or honey if you have a sweet tooth. Just as with everyday tea, which incidentally is made from the dried leaves of a species of camellia, the flowers or leaves can be dried and stored, or in this case they can be used while they are fresh. Make herb tea in the same way as ordinary tea, usually a teaspoonful per person is enough, but this can always be adjusted to suit your own taste.

These teas make excellent night caps. Some people like to sip them, Chinese fashion, with and after a meal as a digestive. Herbalists believe that taken regularly they gradually build up a resistance to many diseases.

There are many plants used for this purpose, but I am listing here mainly flowers. Many people have tasted jasmine tea, I am sure, since this is often sold in Chinese restaurants. A climbing plant, it is a lovely thing to have growing on your house or to use to cover an old building or a shed. The flowers scent the air so sweetly on summer evenings. If you like a slightly fragrant tea, use jasmine to eke out any China teas you buy.

Bergamot (*Monarda didyma*)

This is a true tea plant. It is also known as Oswego Tea and was made originally by the Oswego Indians of North America. The leaves only are used for tea, but the flower stems and leaves can be used in fruit cups. The tea is said to be so soothing that it soon induces sleep if it is taken at night. The leaves are sometimes added to mulled wine. Both the leaves and flowers can be used in salads, usually chopped, although the individual flowers can be scattered as a garnish. Incidentally, if you find the flavour of sage stuffing too strong for your taste, try replacing the sage with bergamot, fresh or dried.

Bergamot, *Monarda didyma*, makes a sleep-inducing tea and is useful for replacing sage in stuffing.

Chamomile

Probably one of the best known of all flower teas is chamomile, *Anthemis nobilis*, now known as *Chamaemelum nobile*, and *Matricaria recutita*, once known as *M. chamomilla*. Both plants grow wild and I have gone into some detail of nomenclature so that you can identify them correctly if you have a wild flower book. If you buy the petals you may be offered double and not single flowers and these are from plants which are grown commercially. They make good tea, but the wild, true chamomile, *M. recutita*, is considered to be the species with the greatest medicinal value.

The plants are wayside weeds and a lush crop of one or the other can often be found growing on land which has recently been disturbed, for instance, on land at the side of new road works. Once the plants flower in early summer, they continue right on until autumn, indeed, I have gathered them in early winter in mild seasons. The blooms can be gathered as soon as they are mature, but not old. The yellow centres should still be well coloured and the petals unreflexed. Nip them from the plant with a fraction of

stem as this prevents the flowers from disintegrating too readily.

Clover (*Trifolium*)

Both the red and white clover make a delicious tea likely to appeal to those with a sweet tooth because ideally it should be sweetened with honey.

Hops (*Humulus lupulus*)

This tea is a good tonic and a digestive and, so I am told, an appetite restorer. Taken hot it induces sleep. It seems to me that an acceptable present for an insomniac friend would be a sleep pillow filled with hops (use a quilted cover for comfort) and a jar of the flowers dried ready for nightcap tea drinks.

Hyssop (*Hyssopus officinalis*)

The shoots should be gathered as soon as they come into flower. Dry them and store in airtight jars to use for tea to help soothe a sore throat or to ease a persistent cough.

Opposite Marigolds on my kitchen windowsill. All of the wholesome flowers look well grouped in this informal way.

Below At any time of the year chamomile tea makes a refreshing drink. Fresh or dried flowers can be used.

Lime (*Tilia*)

Tea made from the flowers of this tree is a favourite with many people. In France it is known as *Tilleul* and it sometimes appears under this name in herb books published in other countries. Gather the whole flower, bracts and all, as soon as the tree is in bloom. Dry the flowers in the dark. Spread them out loosely on sieves or paper and turn them frequently but avoid bruising them or their flavour will not be so good.

If you have an ache or pain or some unaccustomed stiffness (brought on perhaps by climbing a lime tree) make an infusion stronger than that for tea and add it to the bath water.

Marigold

Use *Calendula officinalis*, not the French or African kind. The specific name of this flower indicates its usefulness. It was once used much more widely in cooking than it is today. It can be used in lieu of the much more expensive saffron. The petals dry well and they are among the few kinds of dried flowers which can be bought at stores which sell herbs. These are used in many ways, see page 45. The tea is a digestive. It is also a tonic and helps to clear the skin. Some people use the liquid externally as a skin cleanser and freshener.

The flowers of the lime tree can be dried to make a favourite tea or used to make wine.

Marjoram (*Origanum*)

Tea made from the flowering shoots of this herb is yet another which is considered an effective antiseptic and prophylactic. It is used to ease heavy colds and to soothe sore throats.

Rosemary (*Rosmarinus*)

This tea is made from the dried leaves as a rule, but it is improved, I think, if some flowers are used. Alternatively, add a pinch of lavender flowers. It is said to be good for the heart and for the circulation.

Thyme (*Thymus*)

Sweeten thyme tea with honey and serve it piping hot to anyone with a tickling and persistent cough.

Verbascum or Mullein

Some people swear by verbascum tea and say that it will soothe really bad coughs. Gather the flowers carefully so that they are not bruised and dry them like lime flowers. Use only a few flowers at a time, six boiled in a pint of water for ten minutes or so will produce the right infusion.

Woodruff (*Asperula*)

This native plant is also a good ground cover plant for wild gardens and is one of the best of all tea plants and it, too, is often used to eke out expensive teas, although it is also quite delicious on its own. Gather it when it first comes into flower and dry its flowering tips.

To ease a sore throat try making a tea from the shoots of marjoram. The wild form is shown here.

Flowers for Wine

For many years my husband and I made gallons of wine of all kinds, using roots, fruit and flowers, the favourites among the latter being clover, hawthorn and the comforting dandelion, possibly because these could be found growing on our doorstep, or nearly so since our cottage plot had not yet become a garden. Now our son has become the family vintner. He, too, is surrounded by garden and countryside. His cellar is most impressive and his preparation at some times dramatic, almost theatrical. Imagine a windowsill row of from one to two dozen gallon jars, each fitted with an airlock, all bubbling and gurgling away with their individual brews, their colours ranging from the palest citron through yellows, golds, orange, red and, of course, wine-purple, since he also has access to large quantities of grapes.

The variety of flowers he uses fascinates me as you might expect. Besides those with which we were familiar there are the more unfamiliar kinds such as honeysuckle and lavender among others.

Home-made wines vary considerably. There are always some which after tasting one sets aside for use in cooking, a great economy incidentally, while others make good aperitifs, wine cups and table wines. Most flower wines though have a delicacy or an unusual bouquet that befits them for special dishes and occasions. Being able freely to experiment in this field secure in the knowledge that it is costing you very little to do so is an enjoyable extension of flowercraft and *degustation*, that delightful French word with its implications of lip smacking and gluttony. Recently, at dinner, our son and his wife served us a carob ice-cream and a cooled, fragrant primrose wine to sip with it, a dessert course which was as delicious as it was unusual.

Home wine making is much simpler and surer than it used to be. We used to follow my mother's method of spreading baker's yeast on a slice of toast and floating it on the surface of the lukewarm liquor to start it fermenting. Now you can buy specially prepared yeasts which are simply added to the 'must' or prepared juices. Most large chemists and some health stores have departments where you will find wine, sherry and all-purpose yeasts, sterilising equipment and all else. Below I give a basic recipe which gives the minimum amounts required to make a good, cheap flower wine. It is not for roots or fruits. Like most basic recipes it can be changed to suit your own tastes or pocket. One can, for instance, add half a pound (quarter kilo) of raisins, another lemon or orange, even a little tea. Most keen wine makers keep a record book and I recommend this practice because it will help you retain or improve the quality of a wine from one year to another, seasons permitting.

My son stresses, and I underline, the following points: be certain what flowers you are gathering and follow prescribed kinds; sweet though they may be to look at, not all flowers are good for the stomach. Do not gather flowers from the verges of busy roads, not only will they be dusty but they may be contaminated with lead or other poisons. Do not gather flowers near areas which have been chemically sprayed for any reason. Do not gather scarce wild flowers, make do with others. Incidentally, I have not listed some flowers such as cowslips from which wine was once widely made because of their present scarcity. Others such as primroses can be grown in quantity in one's own garden.

The utensils and equipment needed for flower wines are the same as for roots and fruits. Some are sure to be at hand. After the modest outlay for the others, costs for each successive brew are few. Airlocks fitted into the tops of fermenting jars allow the bubbles to escape while keeping air from the young wine. A corker is a great help when the time comes to bottle the wine for storage.

The sweetly scented honeysuckle flowers make a good and unusual wine.

Basic recipe

Flowers (quantities are packed not loose volume)
1 orange, finely peeled to eliminate pith
1 lemon   „   „   „
2 lb 4 oz (1 kg) sugar
6 pints (3.5 litres) water
1 teaspoon prepared wine yeast

Like the potpourri for which I gave recipes earlier, the quantities of flowers are not really critical. Generally speaking the amount is adjusted according to fragrance. The quantity of sugar can also be varied according to taste, but bear in mind that most home-made wines tend to be somewhat on the sweet side.

Flowers and leaves from which we have made wines and approximate quantities used are as follows: clover, 7 pints (4 litres); coltsfoot, 7 pints (4 litres); dandelion, 7 pints (4 litres); elderflower, $1\frac{3}{4}$ pints (1 litre); gorse, 7 pints (4 litres); honeysuckle, $1\frac{3}{4}$ pints (1 litre); lavender, 1 pint (570 ml) of leaves; may or hawthorn, $1\frac{3}{4}$ pints (1 litre); primrose, 7 pints (4 litres); rose petals, 5 pints (3 litres); yarrow, $3\frac{1}{2}$ pints (2 litres) of flowers and leaves.

Others you might like to try include: balm, melissa, $1\frac{3}{4}$ pints (1 litre) of young leaves or leaves stripped from the flowering stems; broom, 7 pints (4 litres); burnet, $3\frac{1}{2}$ pints (2 litres); chamomile, 1 pint (570 ml); fennel, $1\frac{3}{4}$ pints (1 litre) of leaves; golden rod, 1 pint (570 ml) of flowers; hop, $3\frac{1}{2}$ pints (2 litres) fresh, 1 pint (570 ml) dried flowers; lemon thyme, $1\frac{3}{4}$ pints (1 litre) leaves with or without flower tips; lime, $2\frac{1}{2}$ pints (1.5 litres) fresh, 1 pint (570 ml) dried; marigold, $1\frac{3}{4}$ pints (1 litre) fresh, 1 pint (570 ml) dried flowers; meadowsweet, 7 pints (4 litres) flowers; mint, $1\frac{3}{4}$ pints (1 litre) leaf tips; pansy, $2\frac{1}{2}$ pints (1.5 litres); sage, $3\frac{1}{2}$ pints (2 litres) young leaf tips; snowdrop, 4 pints (2.5 litres); tansy, $1\frac{3}{4}$ pints (1 litre) flowers and leaves; wallflower, 1 pint (570 ml).

Equipment

Large bowl or bucket, not made of metal
Plastic funnel
Large saucepan or preserving pan
7-pint (4-litre) container, bowl, jar or bucket, not metal
Sieve
Cotton wool
Length of rubber or plastic pipe for siphoning
Wine bottles, corks, corker
Airlock
Campden tablets

Method

Why not grow a supply of primroses in your garden for making into wine?

Place the flowers in a large vessel and cover with 5 pints (3 litres) of boiling water. Allow to soak for 72 hours stirring twice daily.

Strain the liquid from the flowers through a non-metal sieve or nylon cloth into a large saucepan or preserving pan. Squeeze the flowers as dry as possible and discard. Add the thin peel of the orange and lemon. Bring to the boil and simmer for 15 to 20 minutes.

Sterilise the fermentation vessel and rinse well with tap water. Pour 2 lb 4 oz (1 kg) of sugar into the jar. Stand the jar on a wooden board and pour in the hot, strained liquid, shaking the vessel to dissolve the sugar.

Plug the neck with clean, sterile cotton wool or tissue and leave to cool to blood heat. Add the juices of the orange and lemon and 1 teaspoon of yeast powder. When cool seal with a sterilised airlock, or alternatively cover tightly with clean polythene sheeting or a washed party air balloon.

After the original vigorous fermentation has ceased, top up the vessel with tap water. If a sweet wine is desired add up to 1 lb (450 g) of extra sugar at this point. Leave, still covered, to ferment until the wine is clear and no longer bubbles. Siphon into sterilised bottles and cork or seal.

This process from start to finish may take from three to eight months depending on several factors, so be patient.

Giving Flowers

For many of us the first flowers we ever give are those we pick when we are out for a walk. Most mothers will recall (and for some it is a delightful anticipation) the tightly held little posies of daisies picked from the park grass and pressed into their hands with the words, 'These are for you!' And what pleasure these first little offerings bring.

As a child, going out with friends to look for flowers in their season, special kinds such as the first coltsfoot, violets, pussy willow, primroses, cuckoo flowers, ox-eye or moon daisies, orchids and bluebells, were all part of country life. I remember how on our way home it was important that we sat down somewhere and with care rebunched our flowers so that each posy of tiny blooms was surrounded by a collar of leaves, usually the flower's own foliage, but quite often large, glossy ivy. Each long-stemmed bunch, often with a special tuft of quaking or some other pretty grasses in the centre, would be wrapped around with fern fronds, their tips rising above the level of the flowers and pointing slightly outwards.

We believed that we were making the bunch more attractive and ready for presentation. Certainly on reaching home it was most likely to have the stems trimmed, should this be necessary, and then would be stood as it was in a vase of water. We did not realise that we were following a traditional custom in the patterns that we made, or that the foliage around them kept the stems cool and protected the blooms as well. We were learning simple flowercraft.

Some children went to much greater trouble and made cowslip balls, loose pompons of those clustered, speckled, scented flowers; trifles which I fear are denied today's children because the flowers themselves are so much scarcer and where they do grow should really be left to seed. Primrose bunches were well collared with their crinkly leaves and tied with long, tough grasses or darning wool secreted in pockets, so that they could be threaded on sticks and then carried, dangling prettily, shown off in fact, between two children, or hung nonchalently over a boy's shoulder. Certainly the flowers themselves suffered less this way than they would have done held tightly in hot little hands.

Small girls decked themselves, and any smaller ones they might be minding, with daisy chains, sometimes several around one little neck so that there were spares to present to sisters at home who had not come on the walk because of some chore. One can still make daisy chains and also daisy branches which are budded hawthorn twigs with the flowers impaled on their thorns.

The joy was in the gathering and in the giving. It was only in later years that we realised and cared how difficult it is sometimes to coax wildings to revive and shine out again with their original brilliance. Nowadays we know that where wild flowers can, without danger to conservancy, be picked, it is best to put them immediately into a plastic bag and to condition them when one reaches home. If you intend to give the flowers away, spend a little time on them first and present them looking as fresh and pretty as when you saw them growing.

Gift arrangements

When you give any flowers, wild, garden or bought, I suggest that you should take a little time and trouble so that your gift will be both enjoyable and memorable. It so happens that you collect a bonus – in making it so special for the recipient, you will also be making it so for yourself.

In some cases, I know, the very act of having to care for and arrange the flowers might be an essential part of the pleasure of being given flowers, but there is another aspect of this to be considered also. It is possible that should the flowers be sent to a hospital, a sick room, or even to one who is presently working all out to prepare a party, what should be a delightful present could become just another chore, and what a pity this would be.

So take a little time, and instead of a bunch send an arrangement. This need not be more expensive, as I hope to prove, but it will be more personal. Indeed, you should be able to tailor the arrangement to suit the person or the occasion. Sometimes this can be great fun, resulting in novel as well as pretty arrangements.

If all the time you are gathering, buying and arranging the flowers you think of the person to whom you are to give them, of his or her preferences for colour, where the flowers are likely to stand, whether scented flowers are especially appreciated or little unsophisticated flowers preferred to the choicer or more flamboyant blooms, and any other little thing that will contribute to the completed design, then you are certain to finish with something quite captivating, and it should be as pleasing to you when it is done as it will be to your friend.

This is not a book about flower arrangement as such, I seem to have written half a hundred of these, but I think it might help any one who has not made numerous flower arrangements if I explain a few points. Arranged flowers should be displayed flowers. In an arrangement or an ensemble each should be given its own space so that all of its lovely outline can be admired. Even when they are massed flowers should not be hidden by each other. Because of this, I suggest that you are likely to discover that you need fewer flowers to make a full, well-furnished arrangement than you do to make a generous looking bunch or sheaf.

Flower companions

This being accepted, what of the flowers themselves? What, in fact, do we mean by flowers? If our arrangements are to be as attractive as we would like them to be, we have to be quite

Stages in making a flower arrangement.
Far left First define the height of the arrangement. Place the tip directly above the centre of the base of the container. You may have to shift the stem base a little to do this. *Centre left* Arrange side stems, more or less at right angles to define width and general style. These can be as wide or narrow as wished, but intermediate stems should fit inside an imaginary line drawn from the top to the side stem tips. *Centre right* It helps to use contrasting shapes, spicate stems with round flowers for instance. Some stems can flow over the rim area. Short ones can be recessed down between taller stems to give body to the design. *Below* Once you have 'sketched' in the general fabric you can add the denser flowers which should lean forward from the back gradually more and more as they reach the lower levels.

An eggshell, supported by a base of Plasticine, makes an unusual container for a group of tiny spring flowers.

liberal in our acceptance and interpretation of the term 'flower'.

You will find that it will help tremendously if you think of flowers in the widest sense. Let the term embrace any part of a plant that appeals to you, or which you think might be useful, be it bloom, bud, seedhead, leaf, berry, fruit, skeleton or even root.

As you would expect, since the accent here is on *flower*craft, I am not suggesting that we let non-floral parts dominate our arrangements all the time. They can be allowed to do so when, for instance, we make Christmas arrangements, or ensembles for Mother's Day or Mothering Sunday, both of which are dealt with later. Instead, I suggest that in the main we use them to play useful and attractive supporting roles. If you glance through the illustrations in this book you should be able to see how many kinds of plant materials can be used not only as an integral part of the arrangement or other design, but also to aid the arranger. There is likely to be no occasion in which they cannot be used in various ways and for different purposes, for instance to support, enhance, contrast or protect the true flowers. They are often needed to give special effects to arrangements, to set a mood, add atmosphere, tell a story or convey a message, even to make a joke.

It is wise always to build up a stock, not only of dried and long-

Street flower traders take a great pride in dressing their stalls. They know what flowers are likely to appeal most at certain times and they give them pride of place. Those which sell fast and need little conditioning, like daffodils, are often left in the market boxes. Others stand in deep water, ready for arrangement.

lasting materials (see pages 166 to 169), but also of special plants which will provide a useful and attractive range of materials which can be gathered as required.

You may perhaps think that it is best to be a flowers-only enthusiast, but I would like to suggest that from time to time you might wish, and you might find it very helpful, to introduce some item into an arrangement which is not botanical. This could accent the occasion, bring a novelty touch or a note of fun, or even extend a gift as when eggs, real or sweetmeat, go into an Easter arrangement, tree baubles into Christmas decorations or a bottle of champagne into a celebratory gift.

Proving that you can make fun of flower arrangement as well as enjoy it, I made this Christmas gift of traditional greens in a blue measuring jug with three enormous mop head 'chrysanthemums' to brighten it.

71

As a firework party gift, try making an arrangement which includes an assortment of fireworks with red and orange coloured flowers and bulrushes. A small rag doll is the guy.

Choosing a container

This same liberal approach is helpful also if it is extended to take in the vessels or containers in which you arrange the flowers. Certainly if you hope to give arrangements frequently you might find it useful to know that there is a whole range of expendable items such as the deep plastic trays in which some foods are retailed, or cream and yoghurt cartons, which can be made to look attractive in simple and inexpensive ways and which are perfect for your purpose. These need to be associated with suitable types of stem holders, but what you spend on these will save you a great deal on vases and those other containers originally intended for flowers.

You may like to choose certain items to hold the flowers which are themselves acceptable as gifts. This way you extend the value and often improve the nature of the gift. I have more to say on this subject in the following section.

Anchoring the flowers

It is important to realise that flower arrangements intended as gifts differ in more ways than one, even if only slightly so, from

those which are assembled *in situ* for home decoration. In the first place the flowers must be arranged so that they can be safely transported and, unfortunately, accidents do happen. I have known arrangements to be overturned or pushed onto their backs. Arrangements are often handled a considerable number of times after they have been presented, and this is particularly the case with little ones which are intended to be examined close to, even held in the hand from time to time. This being so, all the stems have to be arranged in such a way that they stay in position as the arrangement is moved from place to place.

One of the most excellent stem holders for home decoration is wire netting, but since this has to be used with water it really is not suitable for arrangements which have to be transported, because then the water is sure to spill. The water can be emptied out and replaced on delivery, but I think you would find that some stems would inevitably become disarranged, and in any case having to do this takes away a little of the glamour of the gift. Instead I recommend using the modern foamed plastics of which there are basically two kinds, one which is water retentive and one which is non-absorbent. The non-absorbent kind is used for dried flower arrangements and decorations.

These foamed plastic stem holders are on sale in many large

Above A tin can covered by a cake frill makes the container for this gift arrangements.

Below Foamed plastic stem holders come in many shapes and sizes.

Below Fiddlehead fern fronds, little oak 'tree', bracket fungi, gnarled wood, all arranged on a brown pottery plate create a little woodland scene, an unusual and evocative gift for a country lover who has had to spend his day in a town office.

Opposite By contrast, something feminine and sentimental, a handful of wild flowers. Please don't think that I have robbed the countryside. Although many are also common wayside weeds, all of these grow in my garden. If they have not been specially raised but suddenly appear, my attitude is, 'You can stay if you're pretty, rare, or, becoming very important, if you are a host plant to some butterfly or moth'.

stores, garden centres and florist's shops. There are various shapes, including large blocks which can be cut to the required shape or size with a sharp knife. There are small globes, which can be studded with flowers in the manner of a pomander, cones and even ready-frilled posy or bouquet foundations. The latter can usually be bought only from florist sundriesmen.

One of the convenient things about the water-retentive type of stem holder is that the plastic does not have to be enclosed within a vessel. You can, for instance, simply stand it on a saucer or any shallow, waterproof base. The shape will not disintegrate and once it is well charged with water it is quite heavy and will stand quite safely and firmly. With this type of stem holder it becomes possible to devise almost limitless ways of displaying flowers.

The plastic also can be cut and used to fill any container in a more orthodox manner. However, if you care to play around here

Eggs and flowers can be effectively combined in an arrangement so long as you make provision for both. In the basket is a bowl and heavy pinholder ready for the viburnum branches and flowers. The wood wool (actually any other suitable material can be used) is to help raise the level of the eggs. This must be kept out of water or the painted eggs will spoil. As you will see, the water vessel will later be hidden. Begin by arranging a low branch to flow forward just above the rim level.

you can gain rewards. For instance, plastic cut or arranged in such a way that a good portion rises above the rim level of a container will give you the opportunity of making really deep arrangements, with the lowest levels of flowers really pendant. This is because the plastic will hold flowers quite firmly in any position, even upside down. Furthermore, only a short portion of their stems need be inserted, which means that fairly short-stemmed flowers can be used, including many of the gorgeous kinds which because of their lack of stem are seldom seen in arrangements, such as those great rose-like begonias, velvety gloxinias and orchids which can be cut from a spray of many flowers.

One disadvantage, however, is that not all stems will go into the plastic material as easily as others. Those which are firm even if they are slender cause no trouble, nor do any of the woody or fibrous kinds. The most difficult are soft-skinned, wide, hollow stems such as those of daffodils, and very slender sappy stems such as those of primroses. It is usually no problem, however, to prepare the way for any stem or even for small posies or what have you, by first using a firm stem, skewer or cane according to the required size to make the hole. Push it in just as deeply as you want the flower stem or stems to go, remove it, then insert and arrange the flowers.

The fact that stems can be inserted into a medium which is wet is most convenient, but it should be borne in mind that moisture evaporates quite rapidly from the surface of this material when it is exposed to the air and so water should be poured or sprayed onto or around the block each day. When the stem holder is pushed down inside a container, always cut enough away to make a small channel through which you can pour water into the vessel so that the base of the plastic is kept well soaked. The moisture will then travel up through the entire block. Incidentally, when you send or give an arrangement held in this kind of base attach a little note to it explaining that this should be done. Perhaps you would like to make some pressed flower labels or gift cards to keep for this purpose, if so look on page 179.

Transporting flowers

If you have reason to believe that an arrangement might be roughly handled during its journey, merely through force of circumstances, or if it has to be taken a long way, you would be wise to avoid using tall stems because these may snap even though it is possible to wire them. I suggest that instead of making tall arrangements you use shorter stems and place these in low arrangements, using bowls or shallow containers. Little baskets with handles are ideal for this purpose and somehow there is always a real 'gift' appear-

ance about a basket, probably because it can be so easily picked up and moved from place to place without hurt to the contents.

One has to keep in mind the fact that flowers might become bruised in transport, and once they are well charged with water they tend to crack or bruise more easily than when they are comparatively flaccid and dry. They can be protected quite considerably by arranging leaves below them at rim level. Thus, should a hand or any other object come into contact with the arrangement it will be the leaves which will take the first impact, just as they did when we put collars of them around the wild flowers we picked as children. Leaves can be sturdy and tough without being coarse.

Once all the flowers are arranged as you want them, each stem flowing from the base of the viburnum branch but at different angles and in different directions, cover the 'nest' materials with moss and arrange the eggs. If you fear they may become damp, place plastic or cooking foil under the moss.

77

Arrangements on a theme

Low flower arrangements can be as varied as imagination allows, and perhaps I should explain that by low I mean from a foot down to a couple of inches above table level. Small arrangements are often more acceptable than those which are gorgeous but great. If you are ill in bed the latter have to be admired only from a distance, while the smaller ones can be held in the hand from time to time. This can mean a great deal to someone who has been ill or who has been confined to a room or a bed for a long period.

For designs and patterns you can take in the whole range from the very formal to the informal. In winter, early in the year or in autumn you can make a little picture story to tell what is going on out of doors or in the plant world, a burgeoning twig can act as a tree, a little plant, moss, a stone and a few little flowers can complete the scene. Or you can arrange flowers in much the same way as they would be growing in a garden border, that is in little groups, each kind skirted or framed by its own leaves. If the stems of some of these flowers are very fragile, they can be arranged in the hand, then tied and placed in position as a unit after a stem hole has been prepared for them.

To tell of what is going on outdoors in the plant world, simply take a few burgeoning branches from a shrub or tree, some leaves or an entire plant which grows below or near it, and a knot of the earliest flowers, and there you have the full story. Horse chestnut buds, wild arum and leaves, and a few primroses with a little wooden bird are used here.

Top Gifts in miniature. The large white 'rose' at the centre is a pear blossom which defines the scale of the arrangement. Also used are immature cornus buds, nutmeg-scented Buffalo currant and forget-me-nots.

Bottom Arranged in a seashell, brimming over with the scents and sense of summer, an arrangement of tiny *Rosa polyantha*, heartsease, *Linaria* 'Fairy Bouquet' and sweet alyssum.

A lucky heather horseshoe can be made by wiring heather to a wire base. The ribbon completes the effect and makes this a 'good luck' gift which would be acceptable to a man or woman.

You can, of course, make an arrangement following the accepted rules and you can play many variations on this theme. It is possible to use a part of the gift as a focal point. For example, if you are sending flowers to a new mother to celebrate the birth of her baby, a soft toy can form the focal point, with the flowers, in colour harmony of course, framing it. Two or three thicknesses of cooking foil, or a plastic lid from a food tin, laid on the soaked plastic stem holder will provide a safe and waterproof base for the toy.

Some things – ceramics or a bottle of perfume or wine – will not need the same protection. These can actually be pushed into the stem holder so that they will stay in place. It may be necessary to use a slightly larger block than usual; position this on a base, arrange the gift at whatever angle is the most attractive and then distribute the flowers around it.

If you want to use something which might fall over in transit, secure it with a ribbon tied around some part or parts of it and attach this to a rigid cane or skewer firmly inserted into the stem holder. The flower stems arranged about it will help further to wedge it in place.

It is sometimes a problem to know what gift flowers to arrange for a man. You might find it useful to mix objects not only with cut flowers but also with a pot plant or two. The latter can be removed later and enjoyed on their own, on an office windowsill perhaps.

A dish of moss embroidered (or seemingly so) with little flowers is a good way of making an arrangement in the early days of spring when flowers are scarce. The mossy surface can be broken here and there with an uprising group of, say, snowdrops or crocuses, but because the moss itself is very attractive the flowers need not be massed. Bun moss is pretty for this purpose but it is not so common as that which can be gathered from the hedgerow or even the lawn. The latter should be teased before arranging it so that all the dross falls out or can be pulled out. Make a shallow layer of stem holder if you intend standing some flowers vertically, and cover this with the moss, otherwise the flowers can simply be tucked into the moss itself. Make sure that no frond hangs over the rim because this might make a siphon and the water would slowly drip from the container.

On the opposite side of the scale, you can make any number of formal designs. The plastic stem holder can be cut to outline any shape you wish and then covered with flowers; cats, rabbits, fish, hearts, cottages and many other objects come easily to mind. Fish can be best covered by using overlapping leaves like fish scales. The flowers can surround the fish. You might have an angling enthusiast in the family for whom the arrangement could be specially made. Massed flowers will give quite a furry effect if you want to make an animal.

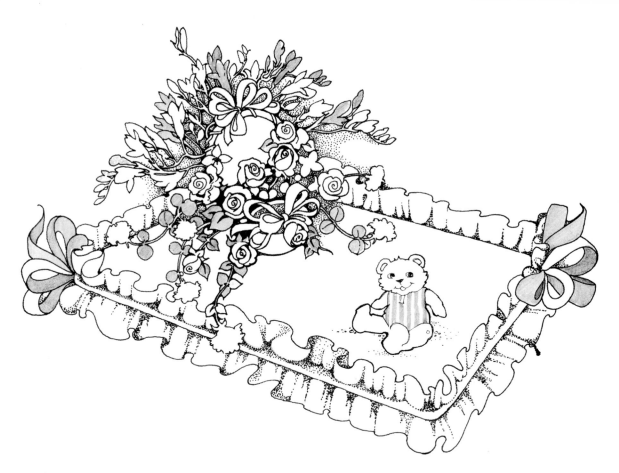

If you cut a round of plastic and fix it into a waterproof holder you can arrange the flowers following the pattern of a Victorian posy, that is, in concentric circles framed by a collar of leaves. In this case, contrary to the way a posy is made with wired flowers, the leaf collar is arranged first. Use small ivy, privet, side fronds of ferns, silvery-grey senecio, variegated elaeagnus, any leaf whose little stem can be easily inserted. When these are in place, arrange the outer ring of flowers against them. Keep heads level. Contrast this ring in colour with the next and continue in this way until the centre is reached.

Traditionally a little rosebud or some other neat, formally shaped flower occupies this position, but there is no reason why you should not give your imagination a free rein and adapt this design to suit a special purpose. You could place a corsage at the centre, something to wear on the special evening out later in the day, or at this point arrange a tiny gift box. Alternatively the arrangement can be large enough to take an important centrepiece. Remember that a great part of the posy area can be filled with attractive and contrasting foliage so that there is no need to use masses of flowers. One 'flower' ring could be composed of some other material than flowers, such as fruit, golf tees even, or you

The birth of a baby is an occasion which offers scope for an imaginative arrangement of flowers. A piece of polystyrene trimmed with ribbon offers a base for the cradle of flowers, which is intended for the new mother, and a toy for the baby.

One of the prettiest and most personal ways of wrapping gifts is to decorate them with some little piece of flower-craft. On the cracker-shaped parcel, yellow helichrysums harmonise with yellow variegated holly and brown fir cones. Below, on the square parcel, honesty has been grouped around fringed gold ribbon to make 'Christmas roses' and beyond these has been spangled with sequins.

could go to the extent of golf balls. Pressed down into the stem holder they will stay in place.

Use this same theme for shapes other than a posy. For first-baby flowers you might make a little crib, with the leaf collar and flowers shaped in the outline of a counterpane laid over a baby doll sitting up against a floral pillow, or better still perhaps, against a sweet herb bag which later can be laid among the baby's clothes.

Arranging flowers for mother and baby can bring much fun and enjoyment. It is a particularly welcome touch if with mother's flowers you include something specially designed for her new baby, even if this is no more than a posy made for the teddy bear or doll you send, a first buttonhole, or a rosebud dressed up with a collar of leaves and a frill of ribbon or a posy of field daisies. Tiny baskets for toys to carry can be made from coloured plastic egg carton sections. Staple on a ribbon handle and fill with flowers.

As I have already suggested, all kinds of useful vessels make good gift containers. If you use baby mugs, porringers, dishes or even certain toys as containers, use the colours in the patterns or the glaze as a guide for the floral colour scheme. You don't have to stick to the traditional blue or pink. And containers need not be made of ceramic or metal. Baby bootees well and safely lined with cooking foil or tiny waterproof cartons of some kind can be filled with flowers very effectively. It is best to secure these to a base and I suggest that a silver-covered cake board, a doily-covered card or a plastic circle will do for this. Staple ribbon to the base and tie each bootee in place.

Floral gift wraps

Linking flowers with gifts can be done in so many different ways and these need not be ostentatious. One of the prettiest ways of using them is as favours to decorate gift wraps to be used at all times of the year, as one would expect at Christmas. These same favours can also be used to decorate crackers, and this is an attractive way to personalise these whether they are bought or made at home.

The basic method of making a favour is to assemble the materials in the manner described for making a corsage bouquet (page 132). Indeed, there are times when a true corsage can be used, on a birthday present or on one for Mothering Sunday or Mother's Day. Generally speaking though, these are little bouquets in which dried flowers are featured, which means that they can be made well ahead of time, a useful point when there are many to be made.

For Christmas the favours can also include tiny baubles, little cones, poppy seed capsules, holly leaves, honesty moons and anything else of a seasonal nature which appeals. Being Christmas, these materials can be given a festive appearance by being glittered or otherwise spangled. For example, honesty moons look attractive if a few sequins are applied to them in much the same pattern as they hold their own seeds in the pod.

A little seasonal garland wreaths a round, paper-packaged Christmas gift. Skeletonised holly leaves, honesty, beechnut cases, larch cones and holly berries are used.

Special Occasions

From time immemorial, festivals have been celebrated with flowers and plants. Used originally as offerings to the gods, these gradually became an accepted and even an essential part of life. At first symbols of many beliefs they later became customary, even conventional, so that apart from altars and temples, on special occasions statues, doorways, homes, tables and even people were decorated with flowers. And after hundreds of years, and usually quite unaware of the significance of what we are doing, many of us still follow the old ways. Yet our modern observance of special dates is a poor thing in comparison to greater glories of the past.

Even so, and happily, the original purpose of using flowers has followed us down the years to today, when we colour and enrich those days we wish to remember. For very special occasions we still decorate our homes and public buildings. More important, I think, we still offer flowers, not to pagan gods but to each other. For many people festivals really are times to 'say it with flowers'. We give flowers, plants and varied decorations, with the emphasis on those for the family table, at Christmas.

St Valentine's Day is not only a date for a traffic in greetings cards, but each year on February 14th more and more flowers are used to speak the language of love.

In Britain the fourth Sunday in Lent is observed as Mothering Sunday, when children pay respect to mother and give her a token of love, traditionally a bunch of flowers gathered by the child, but now more frequently bought. Other countries also observe Mother's Day and in these places a similar custom is followed. Nowadays all children, young and old, are likely to join in this celebration, with father taking this golden opportunity of remembering his wife as well. Even mothers whose children are far away sometimes find themselves remembered by a neighbour, friend or relative.

On this day, as on St Valentine's Day, one finds that the personal element is becoming more emphasised, and this is no doubt due to the greater interest generally in flower arrangement. I find that when in the national newspaper for which I write I feature flowers for Mothering Sunday and suggest ways and means of arranging and presenting them I always get a warm and quick response. There seems to be a widespread desire to get away from the plain bought bunch and to devise some other ways of making mother's flowers specially for her alone so that they are not the same as those everyone else gives. Apart from this, home arrangement Mother gifts are usually less expensive and so within the scope of pocket money or tight budgets.

Easter, like Christmas, is a time to give flowers as well as to display them magnificently in church and generously at home. Decorations are designed to symbolise the return to life, to show that spring has come, and, of course, much of this interpretation

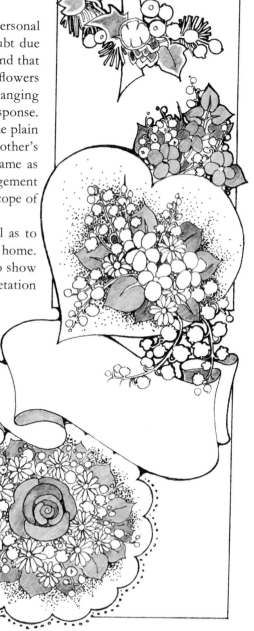

comes from the use of seasonal flowers, particularly if some simple garden or wild material is used with commercially grown blooms.

The dates of Harvest Festival and Hallowe'en tend to merge into each other and certainly similar materials are used in decorations made in celebration of each festival, but where in one the arranger praises and offers thanks, in the other he or she is permitted to show humour, even to play pranks and generally to set the scene for a party. Thus the same flowers and fruits are presented in totally different ways.

If we are to practise flowercraft to its fullest, then there are other festivals to be taken into account, birthdays, weddings, anniversaries and celebrations of all kinds. Nowadays there are so many aids to the arranger that assembly becomes easier and easier as the years go by. Fortunately we shall find that as we learn and practise arrangements and decorations for one date, we shall be all the more skilled and charged with imagination when we come to use flowers for the next. Once skilled in flowercraft you are likely to be asked to help friends to devise floral gift offerings.

Valentines

As one would expect, the theme for Valentine decorations or offerings is the heart. It is possible to buy heart-shaped baskets, baking tins, boxes, dishes and jelly moulds, all of which make splendid containers, as well as the more mundane ceramic and glass ones. It is also a simple matter to cut foamed plastic stem holder blocks into heart shapes. First cut slices of suitable thickness and then use a heart shape as a pattern. Heart-shaped pastry cutters will cut through the plastic. Otherwise take a heart shape, mark around it and then cut down through the plastic with a knife.

Soaked heart-shaped pieces of stem holder can be covered on the base with cooking foil. In fact, if you are deft it is possible to cover the heart on all but the surface and make a silver frill at the same time. Cut a large heart of foil (incidentally, double foil is much more malleable and less likely to split than a single layer), making sure that it is large enough to cover the base and the sides and then turn outwards to make a surrounding edging or frill. If you have them, use pinking scissors to cut this edge so that it can be used as part of the pattern. This method of cutting a shape from stem holders and covering them can be used for many things other than Valentine favours and is worth bearing in mind. It is, for instance, a good way of filling and using any non-waterproofed container, especially those little mesh punnets used for fruit, even though these are now mostly made of plastic rather than wood.

If you would prefer to surround the heart in some other manner,

Left People have always enjoyed massing flowers in the manner of mosaics to observe some special date or to celebrate some festival. In many parts of Britain well dressing is traditional and a part of local life. In other areas, and in Holland in spring, flower heads (predominantly tulips, the flowers of which have to be removed from the plant for horticultural reasons) are massed into gorgeous, vibrant patterns and used to decorate floats in a colourful floral parade. In church festivals flowers are sometimes massed to make long carpets, leading up the nave from the entrance to the altar. All over the world you will find flowers used this way on some occasion or another and it is worth making a trip to see them, for they are always the result of long, painstaking and loving craft.

Above On a smaller scale you can mass flowers for your own little celebrations. Here I have made a wonderfully diverse range of saintpaulias into a floral valentine. Any spring flower could be used in like manner.

doilies and posy frills can be made heart shaped by pinching one portion and pointing the frill, usually best done by making a tuck in the place directly opposite.

It is not essential to make a solid heart. Use a thick, heart-shaped outline which can be studded with flowers and decorated with a spray or a corsage fixed to one portion.

Tiny hearts can be used in a variety of ways, even if this is no more than incorporating them in a flower arrangement as though they were separate blooms; a heart can also be used as a centrepiece. Small hearts can be studded with the smaller and less autumnal-looking dried flowers such as the little daisy-like acrocliniums and gnaphalium. Little hearts made of bent wire and covered with ribbon, perhaps also adorned with a tiny spray of flowers, can be incorporated into gift wrap favours such as those described on page 83.

Mother's Day

Probably the most popular 'give flowers' day is Mothering Sunday in Britain and Mother's Day elsewhere, these days falling on different dates. I must admit to always having children in mind when I write about this day, and because of this I stress that although the finished arrangement should be as attractive as possible, one should be prepared to encourage children to search for and even experiment with all kinds of objects to see whether or not these would make good containers.

A child usually likes the idea that the flowers, which after all are fleeting, should be arranged in something that mother can keep. Such vessels are limitless. They can range from her own special cup and saucer or mug to teapots, basins, oven dishes, measuring

If you wish to mix the practical with the pretty, turn a work basket into a gift flower arrangement. Here I have mounted the reels of thread on wires and wrapped hanks of embroidery wool around them.

No need to go to great expense for Mother's Day or Mothering Sunday gifts. Such attractive little containers can be made from so many expendable items around us. Here a plastic food tray is doily trimmed and ribbon handled. It contains a block of foamed plastic stem holder.

jugs, large ladles, and storage jars. Alternatively, some pretty little ceramic, glass or metal bygone may be found on a junk stall, such as little gravy boats, tureens, soap dishes, and, since the foamed plastic stem holders can be used in this context, a pretty plate or dish to hang on the wall. A new rolling pin could have a foamed plastic block fixed to it cleverly decorated with flowers.

Devising such gifts is a wonderful way of stimulating a child's imagination, and I have more to say on these lines in the section dealing with Christmas arrangements.

A large container need not be filled with flowers. Instead flowers can decorate it in some other way. A new shopping basket, a mixing bowl or a tray, for example, might cost enough in themselves and not allow for further expenditure on a mass of flowers. However, a little flower arrangement can be made at the base of the handle of the basket or on some similar portion of the other items.

Little foil containers which once held food can be used to hold the wet stem holder, and these are easy enough to fasten to the basket handle with adhesive clay, tape or ribbon. Flowers can be arranged in such a way that the container is hidden, one instance in which the use of plenty of foliage is advisable.

A favourite ploy of mine is to convert brightly coloured reels of cotton, hanks of embroidery wool and balls of knitting yarn into 'flowers' and to mix these with real blooms and foliage. Sometimes two things can be used together, wool being wound around reels to make 'roses'. Balls of wool and yarn make gorgeous outsize flowers when each ball is surrounded by large petals made from individual leaves. These can be preserved leaves or shadow or skeletonised ones. False stems can be made of canes or knitting needles – any knitter welcomes additional needles. Leaves can be mounted on pipe cleaners.

Easter

Each Easter sees me devising new ways of using eggs with flowers. One year I spent many happy hours in the weeks before Easter painting eggs with water colours, each with its own wild flower motif. The eggs were then converted into 'baskets' by giving them ribbon handles. Finally I arranged a bough of silver birch just coming into leaf on a heavy pinholder in a deep plate and hung the eggs on this, while posies of little wild flowers were arranged at the base.

Left cook
They
lower
tin lid, t
glued in
built up b
rings of sh
Finally a litt
each shell an
tiny posy of f
are needed, oth
would be hidde.

Above A variation
theme. Trim an egg
the egg-holding sec
Staple a ribbon or fo
firmly to it. Stand the
centre of a doily and st
just below the handle st
it up and over so that the
hidden. Give each egg its
of flower, in posies or sing
stemmed blooms.

Since then I have used eggshells decorated in other ways with pressed flowers, sequins, silver and gold doily portions, ribbons and beads, to name just a few of the materials. These are also made into baskets holding but a few flowers to keep them light in weight – pour just a little water into each shell. These eggs look lovely on a blossom branch. If Easter falls early it may be prudent to gather blossom branches and force them indoors in the home or in a greenhouse.

From hanging eggs in branches I have moved on to piling them in pyramids, following the shape of the flower cones I make. To do this you need a round base, a shallow tin is good. This should be stood on a pedestal cake stand, a comport or some other similarly shaped object so that the cone is raised above table level. Used eggshells (I save the breakfast eggs) should be well washed before use so that they keep sweet.

Arrange the first layer of eggshells upright with a well-defined outer ring until they fill the tin. Put a touch of adhesive on the base of each and hold it in position for a moment or two before arranging the next one. Fill all but those in the outer ring with water to weight them. When you have made one layer make another not so wide in diameter and arrange the shells in this layer in such a way that you do not cover the openings of those in the outer ring of the bottom layer. Take time over the succeeding layers. Wait while you hold each one in place until you are sure that the adhesive is firm. Finish with one central eggshell at the top.

Pour a little water in each egg in the mound. Then arrange tiny posies in each one. Only a few flowers are required in each, otherwise the egg shapes will be hidden.

A simple Easter basket for a child to make employs a prettily coloured plastic egg carton and six empty eggshells. The carton should be cut and the portion made to hold the eggs decorated by fixing a frill around it. Paper can be cut in strips and pinked or scalloped and stuck or stapled on. Alternatively, cut out the centre of a doily and place this on the edge, stapling it in place and making little tucks at the corners. Ivy, or some other neat, long-lasting leaves can be overlapped and stuck or stapled in place so that a pretty leaf edging is made. A strip of plastic can be cut from the other portion of the egg case to make a handle, but as this has to be long enough to span the section with eggshells and flowers in place, two or three equally sized strips may have to be cut and joined with staples, and sometimes there is lettering on some of these sections. For these reasons I suggest that the handle is covered on both surfaces with ribbon or with crepe or patterned paper. Alternatively, use plaited ribbons or strap-like leaves.

Arrangement is simplicity itself. The joy for the child comes from gathering the flowers and putting them in the shells. Make it clear that small quantities only are required and that stems must

An Easter tree: branches of blossom from our hundred-year-old pear (other blossom and tree branches can be used instead) are hung with an assortment of decorated eggs. Some, with firmly glued ribbon handles, act as little baskets and hold water and fresh flowers. Some have pressed or dried flowers on them. Others are jewelled with sequins and encrusted with gold or silver doily lace. Even portions of the prettily coloured plastic egg cases have been brought into the theme. Decorated and empty of egg they act as baskets or they hold broken eggshells turned so that the best side is uppermost. Daisy roots have been lifted from the lawn (what better excuse for weeding?) and with moss hide the pinholder and fill the brown dish.

be short. Say six stems of forget-me-nots, a dozen field daisies, six primroses and only one daffodil or tulip will be quite sufficient. Flowers can be mixed or ones of the same kind can occupy each shell.

Earlier I mentioned decorating eggshells with pressed flowers, but you can also make charming gift eggs by entirely covering a shell with dried flowers. Again, avoid using those with autumnal colourings. Eggs for this purpose can be blown so that they are entire, or if they have been cracked for cooking you can often join them together again. Have ready a crumpled tissue, crack the egg, stuff one side with the tissue and push the other section over the protruding tissue, matching the crack marks at the edges. Hold the two edges gently but firmly together. You will find that the egg white holds the tissue in place. Use a colourless adhesive for the flowers.

Flowers can be arranged around a 'nest' of natural or coloured eggs. The nest is easily made of garden moss laid on a little piece of foil or plastic, or one of the shallow food trays, to lift it well away from the water or moist stem holder used to keep the flowers fresh.

Baskets and wickerwork of all kinds and plastic baskets or punnets suit Easter decorations, and as you would expect, the egg itself is a good container. Apart from natural eggs, those gaily coloured hardboard and other material eggs can be used, but be sure to line them well to ensure that they are waterproof.

93

Wedding Flowers

Since so many weddings take place around Easter time and on
wards when there are masses of flowers available, perhaps this
would be a good point at which to introduce wedding flowers
Methods of displaying flowers on a grand scale, or in novel ways
often employed for wedding flowers, can also be used in arrangements and decorations for the festivals which follow.

Obviously flower arrangements for a wedding, whether they
are in church, chapel, home or some public building, should be
more ostentatious than usual. After all, they are there to be seen
and to help create atmosphere. This means that those arrangements which stand alone are usually best made as pedestal arrangements so that they are raised and can be seen from a distance
Many churches now have their own pedestals which can be used
I do not intend to go into detail on this style of flower arrangement
except to stress a few points. Much of the success lies in the framework of the arrangement, and to supplement actual blooms leafy

A wedding decoration from garden
flowers in colours to suit the occasion.
Silvery, downy verbascum, blue salvia,
cornflowers, yellow gazania and
achillea.

boughs and blossom branches can be used to define the shape, taking the line as high, wide and deep as required. Do remember that if you have undertaken to do many flower decorations, you are likely to be very busy indeed, and so at all times look ahead and plan so that you can prepare or even prefabricate some of them well beforehand. It will save so much time if you have containers ready equipped some days ahead with whatever type of stem holder you intend to use. Where fresh foliage is to be employed this should be well conditioned so that if it is possible you can arrange the framework a day or more in advance and fill in the main fabric later.

Nothing could be more simple, yet more suited to its occasion than this unsophisticated posy of garden polyanthus held in a lacy collar.

95

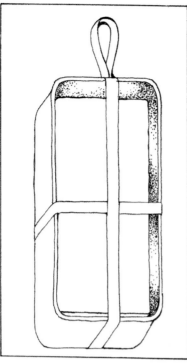

A pew end decoration is easily made from an empty prepackaged food container which holds safely the soaked block of plastic stem holder. Flowers, leaves and any other material can be inserted into the stem holder.

If you intend to make pew end decorations or any similar designs, see that you have foamed plastic blocks cut to size, base-covered and soaking wet.

Do remember that flowers may not be viewed at close quarters and for this reason they need to be sufficiently characteristic as to be easily recognised. Large paeonies, spray chrysanthemums, especially single and anemone-centred kinds, irises (so long as they are not of a blue that melts into the background), lilies, cluster roses, gladioli, large dahlias and chrysanthemums are examples.

If you are making decorations in winter take care that the foliage you use is not too heavy. It is usually necessary to prune away some leaves where these grow thickly or overlap. Those which are ever-green are almost certainly dusty and their appearance is much improved if they are cleaned. For wedding and other parties do not hesitate to use a few whitened or silvered branches with the flowers, but try not to let these dominate. A touch of artificiality is permissible at parties, but first make sure that no prejudice exists. Cycas fronds mounted on long false stems can be used to furnish a party decoration delightfully, especially if these are bleached or whitened and subtly decorated with a sprinkling of sequins or glitter in colours which harmonise with those of the fresh flowers used. Shadow or skeletonised leaves, plain or coloured, fixed into dainty branches, birch or beech, are also airy accompaniments to fresh winter and early spring flowers and like the cycas can be used time and time again. Preserved foliage attractively coloured in light and bright tan, can be kept in store and used frequently in autumn and winter arrangements.

As suggested for Easter decorations, it is often prudent to gather a mass of early-flowering tree and shrub branches to have in hand for such arrangements. These can be cut at any time after the shortest day so long as the temperature outside is not freezing. Split the stem ends upwards with secateurs and stand the branches in two or three inches (5 to 8 cm) of boiling water. Let them remain in this until it cools and then stand them in deep cold water in a warm place indoors. If you want to hurry them along spray the branches with clean tepid water from an atomiser each day.

Unless a wedding is held near Christmas, in which case one might be justified in emphasising the seasonal themes, most ever-greens are usually too heavy for wedding decorations. I have in mind green laurel, spruce, pine and yew as examples. On the other hand, pittosporum and box are dainty and rosemary and myrtle are traditional wedding greens. Some of the variegated kinds can look delightful also and these blend prettily with the white, cream and pastel tints of the flowers usually favoured. Silver-leaved foliage is also acceptable, but take care that the felty leaves of some kinds do not make a siphon and draw the water from the containers onto the table surface. Strip all lower leaves so that none touches water or a damp surface. If you have found that some silver foliage does not take water well, try to cut it with a piece of the old woody stem. Split this and condition it and I believe that you will find the leaves soon become turgid.

Table and buffet decorations

Ropes or swags of flowers for decorating tables can be made in the same way as Christmas swags (page 110), and if you do this allow plenty of time and quantities of materials. You can make a short cut and use less materials into the bargain by using an easily looped material such as ivy, smilax, or even ropes and ribbons for the main line, with foamed plastic studded with flowers at suitable points. You may need only small blocks of the plastic for this purpose. Alternatively, prepare some posies in which the few flowers are prettily surrounded with leaves and/or frills. If these tend to tilt forward simply pin a leaf or stem at the top of the cluster to the tablecloth. Attach loops in the same way.

If the ropes are to go on the apron of a buffet, remember that although the initial impact needs to be really effective, people soon crush against this area, and the materials must be selected with this in mind. If you use some of the less dried-looking perpetuelles, acrocliniums for instance, or yellow and white gnaphaliums (but not, in spring and summer, helichrysums) with plenty of green foliage, these will look fresh and will last well. In summer these can be used fresh this way. Be sure never to use flowers where the petals are likely to shatter easily.

A quick and easy way of making a table or buffet decoration so that the flowers show on entering the room and yet are not likely to obscure the view if people sit at the table, is to arrange the flowers in the necks, or rather on the necks of champagne bottles. Leave labels and neck foils in place. First fill the bottles with water or sand so that they are well weighted. To hold the flowers use either candle cups holding blocks of wet plastic as containers or foil cups, but these must be securely anchored. One of the adhesive clays now available will be suitable for this purpose. Place a ring of the clay around the top of the dry neck of the bottle and press the dry base of the foil cup on it. Turn it upside down to test that it is well anchored. This being so, the flowers can be arranged and trans-ported safely. Alternatively, make a small hole in the centre of the base of the foil cup and push a cork through it and into the neck of the bottle. Decorations not requiring water can be made by push-ing a block of foamed plastic onto the bottle neck or by covering this area with wire netting.

Incidentally, having had to transport so many finished or partly made arrangements to and from T.V. and photographic studios

A quick and easy way to make a buffet decoration is to use a bottle as a pedestal container. First fill it with water or sand to weight it safely. To follow this pattern for fresh flowers and evergreens, first give all a long drink. Prepare the base in advance and add the flowers at the last minute.

97

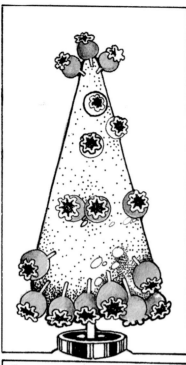

Byzantine cones are delightful and unusual gifts. The plastic base can be obtained in a cone shape and the chosen form of decoration is inserted as shown here. Completed cones can be seen on pages 162 and 168.

and then hand them over to one or more people not always used to treating flowers with great respect, I find that blocks of foamed plastic are invaluable when travelling with flowers by car. Not only can you sink a container into the plastic so that it stands upright, but you can also lay the arrangement on its back and push part of the container into the plastic so that the flowers are lifted from the floor of the box and yet still stay in place. The block that holds the arrangement should be firmly wedged with other blocks to hold it in place and with a block below the flowers to cushion any bumps. It is possible sometimes to place more than one arrangement in a box this way, raising one higher than the other.

Wedding anniversaries

Once a wedding has taken place, wedding anniversaries can be marked with flower gifts with the emphasis placed on the particular anniversary. The imaginative and resourceful will soon find materials suitable to the occasion and so I think it only necessary to note that silver and gold seem to be the most celebrated. No matter what time of year, it will be permissible to use a little glitter, some sequins, baubles or what you will, should the design or the atmosphere call for these. Often the whole scene can be set by simply making a table decoration and adding silver or gold candles and supplying a silver or gold doily-covered base on which to stand the arrangement.

If you decide to use glitter this need not be vulgar, although I feel I should warn you that it can so easily be overdone. Glitter can be applied lightly to the margins of shadow leaves or to white-and-green or yellow-and-green variegated leaves according to the occasion. Usually these look more acceptable in winter and early spring than they do in summer. Silver and gold sequins are somehow softer and more pleasing than glitter and these can be used as discreetly as a court beauty once used patches on her face. Silvered or gilded barley, the ears only very lightly brushed, looks extremely effective and seems to go with every kind of flower, while oats also seem to suit some kinds.

In my opinion Byzantine cones can take their place on these occasions. They offer an unusual shape and not many people can boast of having received a cone of flowers or flowers and fruits, so you can really go to town on this design. You can, in fact, use dried flowers at any season and so present something which can be kept for years if wished.

This is a good design to use for a 'wooden' wedding anniversary. However, these same materials can so easily be silvered or gilded. It is not always a good thing to arrange the cone first and spray it lightly last of all. Paint spray alone can be harsh and very artificial in appearance. You will find that the finished arrangement is much more lovely and dainty if you treat the components individually. Poppy heads, for example, can be very lightly brushed with gold or silver glitter. Yellow strawdaisies can be given a sparkling sequin centre. Honesty moons will take a silver margin or sequin polka dots. Cones can be coated all over or simply given a pretty tip, and so it goes on. Tufts of narrow looped ribbon can be introduced into a flower cone to emphasise the gold or silver theme and the base of the cone can always be decorated with a collar of leaves lightly touched with gold or silver as well. It goes without saying that the container also should help to set the scene, and there are plenty of excellent plastic 'silver and gold' containers.

You could make this a very special golden wedding anniversary gift by gathering the roses from your own garden and drying them yourself. It would be wonderful if they could be the recipient's favourite variety and once they were dried it would not matter at what time of year the anniversary date fell. These are arranged with lonicera sprigs on a foamed plastic globe with a thicker branch as a stem. Arrange the foliage first. Recess shorter, stocky pieces to hide the holder.

99

Harvest Festivals

At harvest time one naturally combines the flowers with the fruits of the earth and there is no reason why one should not also include all manner of other natural things such as bread, shells and minerals. To emphasise the spirit of the occasion it helps to use as containers such vessels as are or were until recently used in some way in the harvesting or in the preparation of food, for example, baskets and trugs, all kinds of measures, wooden, metal and ceramic. With these suitable agricultural or domestic bygones can be incorporated so long as they help create the right atmosphere, although much depends upon the community in which these decorations are to be displayed. Fortunately modern stem holders and foil and plastic linings enable us to use a greater variety of objects than would once have been possible.

I was delighted when I visited a friend in her Canadian home at festival time to find a table decoration consisting of an attractive basket made of plaited dough as a container. She had well baked it to a brisk brown. It was glazed and dry and sturdy enough if kept carefully to serve again for another year, and perhaps even longer.

Nothing so quickly conjures up an impression of harvest as any kind of cereal. Wheat, oats, barley and maize are all attractive in their own way, whether used with other materials or grouped on their own. Stalks of cereals can be mounted on a foundation of foamed plastic or a piece of mossed wire netting to make symbolic sheaves, following the traditional outline, which can either be stood upright or fastened to a backcloth or wall. Stalks and small bunches are easily 'hairpinned' with short lengths of thick florist wire bent double. Take small bunches and begin by making the top of the sheaf. The heads of the cereal should come well above the foundation. Work downwards, laying two or three rows of bunches one on the other so that the heads form a good part of the top of the sheaf. Keep stems neat and uncrossed. Work inwards as you go so that a 'waist' is formed about two-thirds down the sheaf. At this point begin arranging bunches of stem ends only with their bases pointing downwards. Work gradually outwards so that the base of the sheaf is wider than the top. Trim the stem ends level. Finish off by arranging a swathe of corn at the waist to hide the joint and further decorate the sheaf. The quickest way to do this is to hairpin individual ears of cereal arranged to resemble a cable or plait.

Sweet corn can be made into swags. The multi-coloured Indian or Squaw corn is handsome when arranged this way. Pull back the papery shucks and wire or bind these to a foundation rope. Begin at the base with one cob. Above this arrange two cobs so

that they cover the joint of the first. Continue using one, two or three as required until the full length required is covered. This type of swag becomes quite heavy, so work on a table or on the floor. Decorate the top with open corn heads, with their shucks pulled back and separated to resemble flower petals. Some of the smaller varieties of corns such as the Strawberry Popcorn, and any cobs which have not fully developed into large specimens are good for the flowers. Incidentally, one of the best ropes for a swag of this kind is made from one or two nylon stockings. Tightly rolled newspaper is also suitable.

Open corn husk 'daisies' are useful in outsize arrangements, where sunflowers and their seedheads also look in place. In decorations on this scale you can use tall pampas grass and any great leaves such as gunnera and whole cabbages. The red pickling and the ornamental flower cabbages look particularly splendid.

Swags of leaves – evergreens, preserved autumnal or pressed fern for example – decorated with seedheads, fruits, berries, gourds, wild clematis, hops, strawdaisies and physalis can be used

If you are helping to decorate a church at Harvest Festival time, long arrangements on the windowsills and ledges can be most effective.

attractively to wind around a pillar of a church or to decorate the wall behind the buffet at a Harvest Home Supper. Often it is easier and quicker to make these swags in sections and then to place them as though they were unbroken. If the right materials are selected, all of these can be assembled well ahead of the event.

The style of arrangements designed for table centres can be used to decorate windowsills and ledges in churches, choosing an all-round style for those which will be looked down upon, but facing the flowers out only one way if they are set above eye level. In some cases one long arrangement (which might comprise three or more troughs set side by side, using gingerbread tins, for instance) can be placed in the centre of the sill with taller arrangements on each side of it to carry the line up the wall or to frame the base of the window and knit the whole decoration into a unit.

Pew ends can be hooked in place. Bend a length of strong galvanised wire like a meat hook. Push one end up into the foamed plastic block, mossed ball or wire netting and cover the other end with florist tape or ribbon of some kind and then arrange the materials. See illustrations on page 96.

Vegetables are sometimes difficult to group unless they are treated in some way. If you want them left absolutely untouched, they can be displayed by standing them in cream cartons, flower pots, serviette rings, pastry cutters, jam jars or food tins, such devices to be hidden later by materials arranged below. They can be raised further by standing one of these holders inside the other or upon an upturned fellow. As a rule one needs to stand only a small part of the surface of an object in the neck of any of these holders. Solid fruits and firm stems can be gently but firmly pushed into blocks of foamed plastic, and usually a combination of several holders will solve any problem. Those fruits, vegetables and fungi which are to be part of arrangements and used like flowers can be given false stems of wires or canes. Cocktail sticks can be used for subjects such as mushrooms and for lengthening the short, thick, succulent stems of cabbage leaves and some fruits. Many of the suggestions given above can be adapted for Hallowe'en and even later at Christmas. Obviously one would not use a witch or imp theme for any harvest decoration that was to be associated in any way with a sacred ceremony.

Hallowe'en

For Hallowe'en decorations, traditionally the accent is placed on pumpkins and any of the pumpkin family, used in combination with flowers and other materials. These can either be part of a group where they make splendid focal points to a composition, the

pretty scallop-edged custard marrow looking like a great thick flower, the striped gourds placed so that they are almost dartboard patterned, or they can be employed as containers for many other materials. For these, hard-skinned really ripe fruits should be chosen. It is best to cut a slice from the fruit at whatever point you want – this is usually the most difficult part of the operation and I have one acquaintance who always uses a saw to make the cut. Then scoop out the flesh so that this can be saved and used in cooking; it can be replaced with a stem holder of some kind. However, all other kinds of fruit and vegetables may also be used and with them real autumnal flowers, including helichrysums, physalis, honesty and masses of berries.

Candles are a great part of Hallowe'en decorations and these look well with flowers. On this occasion all kinds of fruit and vegetables can be used to hold the candles. Small or large gourds can hold a candle in a small hole cut into them, or they can be entirely scooped out, if you wish with a face made by boring or cutting the requisite holes, and the candle placed inside so that the light shines dramatically through the apertures. Swedes or any other large turnip can be transformed into illuminated faces or some other novelty in the same way. Secure these by slicing the bases and rest them on a Toby-frill collar of flat leaves.

I like to use pineapples as candle holders. These are stood in glasses as eggs are in eggcups. First, though, the glasses are filled with water to weight them and a small doily, with a piece cut out from its centre, placed on the rim around the pineapple. The candle is then fixed into the pineapple centre right inside the leaf tuft. Any of the adhesive clays will hold this, or you can put a piece of foamed plastic inside the leaf tuft and push the candle down into this, a safeguard, incidentally, if it is well soaked with water. It is quite simple to make a wreath of flowers around the base of the pineapple merely by pushing the flower stems through the spaces in the doily into the water below. Cabbages also hold candles attractively and their outer leaves can be bent back and filled with flowers.

When choosing flowers and other materials for Hallowe'en, concentrate on the imp colours, scarlet, orange and yellow, with bright greens if these are used at all, and plenty of sombre shades, browns, blacks and charcoal.

Much of the atmosphere can be instantly created by the accessories which are used, and this I feel is a matter for individual ingenuity rather than flowercraft, so let us tear off the leaves from the calendar and move on to Christmas decorations with the advice that much of what is described as suitable for this festival can be adapted for use at all other times.

Christmas

When we plan Christmas decorations, green, red, orange, yellow and white are the traditional colours to use. Holly, mistletoe, spruce and ivy are the important evergreens, although in fact a greater variety is used, along with some flowers. At one time these were limited mainly to hellebores or Christmas roses and early narcissi such as Paper White and Soleil d'Or. Now, fortunately, each year the selection of fresh flowers available grows wider and their inclusion in Christmas decorations more popular. Entire pot plants are also sometimes used. There are so many other acceptable items which can be used to complement them, that actually in those arrangements which call for fresh flowers, very few real blooms need to be used if they are displayed with thought.

'Snowflakes' made from cycas leaves arranged in blocks of foamed plastic are a pretty Christmas decoration.

While some people insist on having only natural plant materials about them at Christmas, there are others who have a more liberal attitude and will accept all types of accessories and containers. These include figures of Santa, reindeer, snowmen and angels, tree decorations and baubles generally, dried flowers and seedheads and plant skeletons, often glittered or sequined. Candles also play an important role and these are not necessarily intended for lighting; often they are used simply to provide atmosphere and colour. When they are to be lit, however, they should be placed well above any dry materials and they are best used in water or with water-soaked plastic stem holders.

As one would expect, pine cones, holly and ivy berries play their part. Mistletoe can be used, but it needs so much grooming to make it worthwhile in flower arrangements that I suggest it is best reserved for pendant decorations.

The basic cone shape of the Christmas tree seems a natural design to follow for decorations and arrangements alike. It is possible to buy several sizes of plastic cone shapes to use as foundations, or alternatively one can cut cones from small mesh wire-netting and fill these shapes with moss and/or crumbled stem holder, a good way of using up pieces which have become perforated with constant use.

I have one pattern which I often follow of a Christmas tree made of mixed snippets of evergreens and decorated like any other tree with baubles and even tiny gift packages. These trees can be 'growing' in pots. The cone is first fixed onto a stout cane as a short trunk. This must be inserted to about a quarter of its length. If the cane goes deep into the flower pot the tree will be well anchored. The holder for the stem can be foamed plastic, but often this is not weighty enough and it will be found that plaster is best. If the pot or any other container is lined with cooking foil the whole mass of plaster can easily be lifted out when the arrangement

Candles create a Christmas evening atmosphere so well. In a window they call welcome, on a table they bring a cosy, around-the-hearth touch. When candles are part of an arrangement and are to be lit, make sure that they stand well above the other materials. Otherwise, simply let them play a decorative role and enjoy their colour and implication. Arrangements made in water-soaked foamed plastic stem holder kept constantly moist remain fresh throughout the holiday. If the stemholder stands well above its container it gives you a greater area in which to insert the stems. They can also be inserted at an upward angle so that the material flows downwards attractively. When a pair of arrangements are to be made, assemble them together. For instance, when you place a stem to the left, immediately arrange its fellow to the right, so that they end up evenly matched like a pair of gloves. Bells and tree baubles are used with evergreens here, but real flowers or little fruits could play the same decorative role.

This hanging boss is made from evergreens, mistletoe and Christmas bells.

is finished with. The stem should be inserted as the plaster is drying and it may have to be held upright for a while until it stands firm and vertical. A pair of trees of this kind look delightful in a hallway, each side of a door. You can make a tree much larger than its cone foundation would suggest by using longer stems or by mounting short stems on long, thick wires.

Smaller trees can be made as buffet decorations and I find that it is both easy and convenient simply to fix the cone on a bottle neck. Usually only pressure is needed, but it also sometimes helps if a small hole is first made in the centre of the base of the cone. The bottles should be weighted; water will do.

Another simple kind of tree is made by selecting a well-shaped branch of spruce which resembles a Christmas tree in outline – a branch tip is ideal for this purpose. This can be arranged upright in a container and decorated as though it were, in fact, a little tree. It can also be fixed to a backcloth, a rectangle of scarlet felt for example, and used as a wall hanging. Again the branch tips can be decorated and a star or angel placed at the apex.

This same tree-shaped branch is a good backing for most Christmas flower arrangements which are to be stood against a wall and viewed from the front only. The branch can, if desired, be lightly glittered before arrangement. Starry flowers such as anemone-centred chrysanthemums, narcissi and poinsettias (in which case it is best to use an entire small plant) are well displayed against such a background. These can be contrasted and supplemented with baubles and glittered pine cones.

Hanging bosses can be made from evergreens either mixed or all of one kind. As these will not have their stems in water and will also be hanging in the warm upper layers of air, they should all be long-lasting types. The foliage is used to cover the surface of a globe, pomander fashion. (I should perhaps point out that this design can be followed in autumn with dried flowers and orange physalis and cereals for party decorations, and in summer when lavender flowers and sprigs of lavender foliage can be used to make a lavender pomander, an acceptable summer gift.) Globes of foamed non-absorbent plastic can be bought and globes can also be fashioned from wire netting filled with moss or crumbled foamed plastic.

Woody stems should be cut on a slant so that they penetrate the surface of the plastic easily. Frail-stemmed subjects should be mounted on wires. When the boss of foliage is completed the surface should be decorated with small cones, individual physalis lanterns, helichrysums, berry sprigs, lightly glittered ivy berries, baubles, tiny ribbon loops, gilded acorns in their cups, poppy heads and other seedheads in variety. Some of these should first be mounted on wires.

Even small bosses consume a surprisingly large amount of

108

foliage, often much more than is anticipated. Where such materials are scarce, use a white foamed plastic globe and make a feature of the globe itself by transforming it into a decorated snowball. First divide the globe into sections with ribbons. Pin these in place at the poles. Provide a suspension ribbon by extending the ends of one of the ribbon lengths used. The spaces between the ribbons should be decorated in some way. You could use a pressed leaf, a

An arrangement of Christmas evergreens and baubles puts a welcoming touch to the front door. The sprays of fir are first tied together and the other materials are inserted into a block of foamed plastic fixed onto the centre of the fir 'tie'.

Christmas motif of some kind or a row of sequins in each space. Arrange further decoration at the poles. One way of doing this quickly and easily is to use two or three ready made gift wrap bouquets, described on page 83, and simply pin these in place.

All hanging bosses are improved if they are given a little pendant decoration. This is where the mistletoe comes into its own. A sprig can be tied with a ribbon and pinned into the globe at the south pole. Add a ribbon streamer or two, and, if you have them, one or more bauble tree bells which will tinkle prettily as the globe moves in the slightest movement of air.

Many Christmas decorations are hung on walls and doors or placed in windows. Obviously these should lie flat if they are to rest against a flat surface. Garlands can be constructed from hoops of tightly rolled newspaper, wire or wood. If these are covered with red or green crepe paper ribbons, it will not be unsightly if a little of the foundation should show through. Furthermore, the stems which are to be tied to these foundations hold more securely against a rough surface.

If snowflakes are made, their components should be counted in six, although this is not so important for stars. Construction is much the same. Spruce branches, pressed bracken fern and cycas leaves look well and they can be arranged in blocks of foamed plastic or wire netting. Once the points are in place the centre part can be designed and filled in. When making pendant decorations, remember to provide ribbon, rope or string for their suspension early in the assembly.

Swags and garlands

Swags or ropes of evergreens to be draped above mantelpieces, sideboards and buffets, or to hang at the sides of a doorway, can be made by tying small bunches of evergreens to a rope made of tightly rolled newspapers, old nylons or even lengths of cloth. If they are to be looped it is most helpful to make these ropes in sections, for example one or two lengths for the centre loop or loops, with two ropes, one for each side. Hide the joins by clusters arranged separately. Select well-shaped, tapering pieces for the rope terminals. Begin at these points and work towards the join area. As one bunch or stem is bound to the rope (make two twists) lay the next in position so that its tips just cover the twine of the one below it. Pull the twine or reel wire quite tightly because the stems tend to shrink as they dry. If you wish to decorate the greens, mount the decorations and arrange them after the swag has been completed.

Cones can be used this way, in which case their mount wires should be bound to the rope. These look very attractive if short lengths of evergreens and clusters of holly berries are arranged among them.

Opposite A country walk, or a search under trees in a park, will usually provide plenty of materials for Christmas garlands. Larch cones, beech nut cases, acorns and wild clematis, with a little thuya, holly and mistletoe are used here.

A wooden spoon can be used as a surprise gift or the base for a wall ornament. Attach a piece of foamed plastic stem holder to the handle and arrange the stems in this.

Novelty gifts

As Christmas is such a time for giving, you might consider dressing up really practical items with flowers and Christmas greens in such a way that they can be used as Christmas decorations during the holiday and then pulled apart and put to use afterwards.

Dustpans might not immediately present themselves as eminently suitable subjects for flower arrangement, but I can assure you that they are surprisingly versatile and they come in pleasant fresh colours to which their contents can be matched or harmonised. Furthermore, most stand firmly on end. They will fit neatly on a shelf, which means that you can make an attractive mantelpiece or bookshelf decoration in them.

Whether you use fresh flowers and foliage or a selection of dried materials must depend upon whether or not the container is waterproof. Most dustpans will hold water. If you buy a dustpan and brush set, the one is usually fixed to the other. Let the brush remain in place, it is quite pretty in its way, and simply bring it into the general design.

Measuring jugs and basins, especially if these are opaque or coloured, make good contemporary containers and many people would welcome a new one with metric measurements. Flowers for them need not be fresh and real, although these always look good, they might be more fun if they are fantastic. You can, for instance, make fantasy 'blooms' from wooden spoons by surrounding the spoon end, the flower centre, with petals made from real leaves. These can be fixed to the back of the spoon with tape. Alternatively, mount each one on a wire and bind the 'stems' together under the spoon end where they are hidden by the lowest petal.

Like most pretty, useful presents, wooden spoons can serve as Christmas decorations, as wall ornaments for instance. First tie a bright suspension cord or ribbon near the end of the handle and then decorate the spoon around the bowl area. Arrange a little spray of evergreens in the hand, tie it and attach it to the spoon with tape, or to get the best result first tie a stem holder to the spoon.

Use either a walnut-size ball of crumpled wire netting or a little block of foamed plastic attached with sticky tape or string near the base of the handle. Arrange the stems in this as you wish, working from the outside inwards to the centre. The stems should flow easily in any direction and they soon lock and hold fast.

If you want to add baubles it is best to use the unbreakable kinds. Mount these and any other stemless objects on wires, pipe cleaners or the wire-spined bag fasteners usually found in packets of plastic bags, or if they can be inserted easily, on cocktail sticks.

As a present for the keen cook use fresh bay leaves instead of spruce and holly. Make *bouquet garni* 'apples' to mix with garlic and shallots instead of flowers and baubles. Push a clove into the centre of a round *bouquet garni* bag to make the apple's centre. Fix two or three bay leaves behind it.

Tea towels can be used to make really handsome decorative gifts. I like to frame them so they can be hung up like pictures. They look good hanging on a door to a room. I decorate these with sprays of greens, dried flowers, physalis, cones and baubles, or whatever seems suitable and harmonises well with the colour and the character of the pattern on the cloth.

The frames for these pictures are easy to make, but they have to be stitched on, not an onerous task for long stitches will do quite well. Make long, thin spills of newspaper, cover them with brown crepe paper cut into strips which can be wound around the spills, and stitch them to the top and bottom of the towel. Cut and neaten the spills at the towel edges. Alternatively, fix a frame to all four edges. Stitch on a ribbon or a cord in the top centre to suspend the towel. At this stage, to hide the stitching and where the frames cross at the corners, or at any other point you like, attach the sprays. These are best stitched on in such a way that they can easily be pulled off after the holiday when this particularly pretty, useful present is put to use. It is possible to buy pairs of end frames for towels and posters alike. Made of plastic, these can be simply slid along the top and bottom edges. The top has a suspension cord.

Gifts can be practical as well as pretty. Here is an example for someone newly setting up home. An almond-green dustpan and brush, the handle portion of which is decorated with pink carnations, a rosette of chlorophytum leaves and a few cuttings of rhoicissus, included not only to complete the little arrangement but also to start a house plant collection, since they can so easily be rooted in water.

A *cordon bleu* garland I designed as a special gift for a keen cook. Fixed to a ring of plastic wire netting are 'apples' made from *bouquet garni* bags, each with a clove centre, golden shallots, bay leaves and, naturally, blue ribbons.

Right A variation on one of my favourite Christmas themes, the tree or conifer shape. A foamed plastic cone has been pushed onto the neck of a weighted bottle. Snippets of holly and various evergreens, dotted with cones, cover the shape. Finally, tree baubles and false lighted candles bring it aflame.

Wiring Flowers

Although the simple flower arrangement, especially of the recipient's favourite flowers, is sure to be welcomed on any occasion, there are times when a little extra effort or some unusual theme, or style, or interpretation is called for. In order to make a wide variety of floral arrangements, whether these be for gifts or for some other purpose, some knowledge of professional floristry is helpful.

There are many people who dislike the thought that flowers have to have wires inserted in them, but we should bear in mind that if flowers are to be transported, or simply held in the hand for some time, they have either to be supported by having their stems wired, or their stems must be removed and replaced by wires, otherwise heads are in danger of being severed from their stems.

The use of wires also ensures that flowers and all parts of plants can be modelled in styles or displayed in ways which would not be possible if the stems were simply stood in a vessel of water. When bouquets for weddings or presentation have to be made, the large or complex and polyanthus types of blooms may have to be divided and wired so that they will be neither too large nor too heavy. Often the stem of a large bloom is very heavy and where several are used in a design it could become too heavy to be held with comfort for more than a few minutes. The same applies to those flowers which are to be worn and which must be dainty and

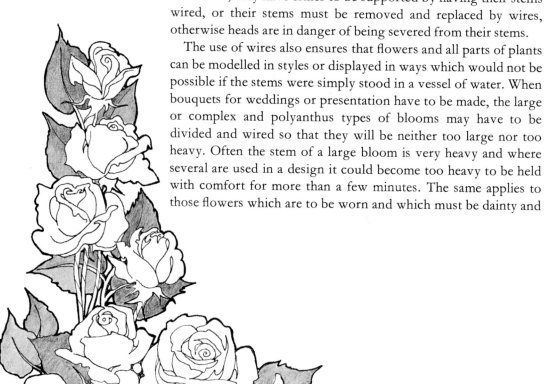

light in weight. If they are not they will look unattractive and they could also tear or pull out of shape any material on which they have been pinned.

Not only flowers but other plant materials which are to be arranged with them also have to be wired. Leaves will not remain turgid, or cannot be curved, or perhaps placed in the right position unless they are reinforced in some way. A certain amount of wiring is also needed for dried flower arrangements, Christmas novelties and other festival flowers.

Of course, most of the flowers we use everyday will need no wires – indeed, the less these are handled the better as a rule. However, the arranger will find that once he or she learns to handle florist wires skilfully and thus neatly and inconspicuously, there will be occasions when a wire or two will be of great assistance in more ways than one. A wire inserted into a bent, damaged stem can result in a flower being used decoratively instead of being thrown away. A wire inserted a little way up into the end of a short stem can transform an unimportant flower into one that can play a more useful role in an arrangement. A wire added to the short stem of a leaf can mean that all kinds of individual leaves, so often overlooked, can be used in ordinary flower arrangements. A wire can be applied to a too-straight stem in such a way that the stem can be coaxed to assume a gentle and more attractive line.

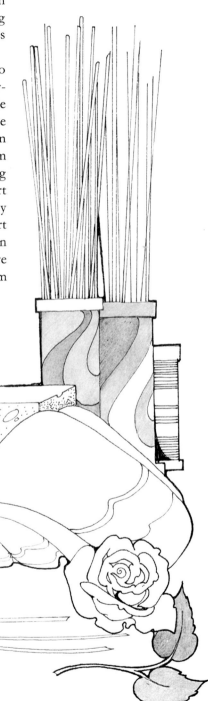

Types of wire

Wires, which are sold by florist sundriesmen and sometimes by friendly and obliging florists, come in various lengths and thicknesses and are sold accordingly.

I should point out that these were once sold in lb, inches and gauges and in case there should still be stocks in this category I have shown how the gauges have been replaced so that the wires now conform to the metric system of measurement.

The unit of weight is based on £X per 25 kg. The weight of each bundle, irrespective of gauge, is $2\frac{1}{2}$ kg. Florists sometimes will sell smaller quantities than this to customers who are not likely ever to use an entire bundle.

Sizes are:

1·25 mm replacing 18 gauge
1·00 mm replacing 19 gauge
0·90 mm replacing 20 gauge
0·71 mm replacing 22 gauge
0·56 mm replacing 24 gauge
0·46 mm replacing 26 gauge
0·38 mm replacing 28 gauge
0·32 mm replacing 30 gauge
0·24 mm replacing 32 gauge
0·20 mm replacing 36 gauge

All wires are available in the following lengths.

90 mm replacing $3\frac{1}{2}$ inches
130 mm replacing 5 inches
180 mm replacing 7 inches
230 mm replacing 9 inches
260 mm replacing 10 inches
310 mm replacing 12 inches
360 mm replacing 14 inches
460 mm replacing 18 inches

Opposite If you count them, there are really very few flowers in this bouquet. There are white, bell-like, waxy lapagerias, unusual rosy-pink arums, daintier perhaps than one imagines these particular flowers to be; scented, wax stephanotis, the 'Bride's Flower'; freesias and lily-of-the-valley. These last two are wired the full length of their stems. The others are all mounted in various ways according to their weight or textures. A bride should be able to carry a bouquet with ease as well as with dignity, so it is most important that it should be well balanced. One should test this while assembling the design. For good balance I have kept the greatest weight at the centre and then gradually tapered the flowers from this area without isolating the centre zone. A little green at the back of a bouquet helps it to stand out from the fabric of the bride's gown. I chose to use the garden arum leaves because of their association with the rose-coloured kind from Kenya.

Wires should be stored in the dry, preferably wrapped in lightly oiled paper or in a plastic bag the inside of which has been wiped over with oil, because they will rust quickly. Actually, so far as wiring the flowers is concerned, this is an advantage. The wet sap which comes in contact with the wire will cause it to rust quickly. This means that the wire remains secure. This applies to wires which are inserted into the centres of flowers or up into their stems. Where it is not desirable that wires should rust and show some stain on flowers or leaves, so-called 'silver', usually reel wire, is used.

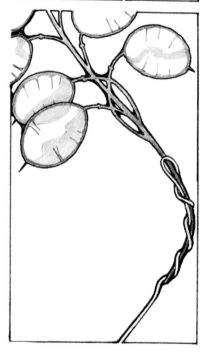

External wiring

Since flowers vary considerably, it follows that they are not all wired in exactly the same manner, and apart from their special characteristics, they are also wired according to the role they have to play. It is, therefore, important to recognise and learn more than one method of wiring.

As I said earlier, some blooms, especially when they are turgid and well charged with water, snap easily from their stems. I remember walking behind a hotel page boy who was taking a basket of roses to a visitor's room and seeing (and picking up) four rose heads from the corridor floor. This beheading was no fault of the page's, the flowers had not been wired – possibly because it was known that wired flowers would not be appreciated. In this case, a little 'cruelty' would have saved the flowers. Wired flowers stood in water last as long as those which are unwired. Therefore, where a flower is to be arranged and is to look as natural as possible, yet is to be transported and possibly handled considerably in some way or another, it is wise to wire the entire stem. This can be done quite inconspicuously.

Examples of flowers to be treated this way are roses, carnations, tulips and single-stemmed orchids. The method of wiring a rose stem can be applied to these and to any other bloom. Obviously, the smaller the blooms and the more slender the stem, the lighter the wires should be. Roses have a seed box under the flower and this has to be pierced with one end of the wire. The wire is then pushed on up into the seed box until it is well embedded. If the wire enters the seed box at a point very near the junction of it and the stem, the wire will hardly show. Use long wires of medium gauge. If you are in doubt at any time select a lighter rather than a heavier wire. The latter is more conspicuous and not so malleable.

Hold the top of the stem, where the wire has been inserted, with one hand and twist the remainder of the wire down the stem, passing it round the stem at the leaf axils. This way it will not show so much. There is no advantage in twisting the wire round the stem several times in the spaces between the leaves. As you take the wire round the stem at the first leaf, let go the top of the stem and hold it next by the leaf. Continue this way until the stem end is reached. Twist it round the base to secure it. Keep the wire as close to the stem as you can all the time. When you reach the end, press it hard against the stem.

One point always to be borne in mind: when cut flowers are stood in water or in some water-retentive material, they go on growing. If there is insufficient wire pushed up into the base of the bloom and if the flower is arranged or simply stood in water for a few hours awaiting assembly, you will discover that the end of the wire becomes free. It is, of course, unsightly and it might also

Above and opposite External wiring gives support to the stems and in some cases allows the stems to be bent.

become dangerous. Supposing that someone should bend over the flowers to smell them? And if the flowers have to be assembled they may have to be wired all over again. So be sure to push the end of the wire up into the heart of the bloom, but take care that it does not then protrude from the centre. Usually you can sense quite easily when the core of the flower has been reached.

Forced tulips are inclined to curve their stems quite considerably once they have been given water. It is best to insert the wire some distance, say an inch below the base of the bloom and then gently to push it up so that it reinforces the top inch or so and also penetrates up into the stigmas of the flower. As the stem grows the wire will remain inside it even though there may not be such a long portion within the stem as there was originally.

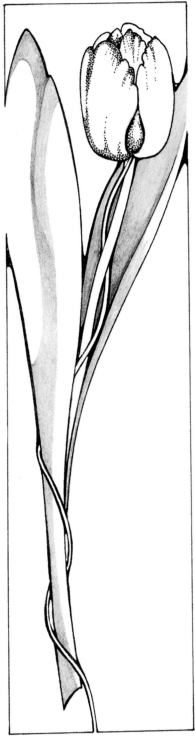

Left Hyacinths, and any firm, bell-like flowers can be threaded like beads onto a wire. They can then be used in many ways in bouquets.

Wires to replace stems

In order to lighten the weight of the finished design it is often necessary to remove all or most of the flower stem. In some cases, roses for instance, it helps if a short portion of stem is left and in cases where it is important to present the flowers looking as natural and as unmodelled as possible, for certain corsage designs for instance – as we shall see – it is best to retain two or three inches (5 to 8 cm) of stem so that an unwired, untaped portion of stem is visible. It takes a little more skill to insert a light wire up into several inches of stem than it does to push it up into a fraction of an inch. Probably this is the reason why some people use a 1·25 mm wire for this purpose, something I do not advise because the resulting design is heavy and stiff. It is much better to practise and practise until the operation is done with ease. Always, try to use the lightest wire possible, if you have to use wires at all.

For roses, use a 0·90 mm wire, 310 mm (12 in) or 360 mm (14 in) long. You can cut it to the required length later. It is better to do this than to use short wires which may have to be lengthened by other wires because this only adds to the general weight. As already explained, the wet sap will cause the wire to rust quickly so that it should remain quite secure, but if you want to wire a large, heavy rose and feel that more support is necessary, you can insert two very fine wires crosswise through the seed box. Bend them downwards so that the four legs which project equally on four sides of the seed box are parallel to the 'stem' wire. To secure these, pull one of the wires out from the rest and twist this round the other three, binding them all to the thicker 'mount' wire. Cut this to the required length.

Above Replacing the stem with a wire.

Right The lovely hues in the centres of the cymbidium orchids and the tints of their outer petals are repeated in the roses and freesias arranged around them.
It is possible to make and use a detachable corsage bouquet as a centre so that part of her bouquet can be worn later by the lady if she so wishes.

Crosswiring

Crosswires are also used to prevent roses from opening wide, often necessary when they are used in posies or bouquets. In this case though, the wires are pushed right through the bloom near the base of the petals. They are then taken down over the seed box – often you can hide them by passing them down through the sepals – to the mount wire. Naturally, the wires should be passed through the centres of the base of the petals.

Carnations and pinks are wired in the same manner, i.e. into the base of the calyx and up into the hard seed box to mount them, and using two crosswires right through the calyx to provide extra security should this be thought to be necessary. Small pinks should be wired with small gauge and lighter weight wires.

Substitutes for stems

While most flowers with firm or rigid stems are best mounted like roses on a stem wire, others need to be treated quite differently. Begonias, for instance, have fleshy stems that will not take a mount wire well – they tend to disintegrate when the wire is inserted.

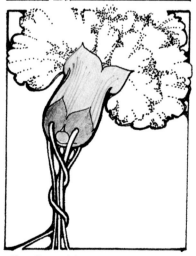

Above Crosswiring

Left Taped wires are neatly bound into a straight, slim handle as they are assembled.

Right The flowers are arranged to frame the orchid in the centre of this corsage. The stems are neatly taped and then tied together below the orchid leaving the ends free.
Opposite After stitching with wire the leaves can be bent and curved as you wish. Here the wired leaves are brought together and bound in place. Later a ribbon is added to hide the join.

Above Wiring a flower with a short stem

These and other flowers like them can be wired as follows: on the outside of the begonia are two petals known as the guard petals. Grasp these at the top and hold the flower between the finger and thumb of one hand. At about one-third of an inch above the junction of bloom and stem, pass a medium weight wire through the bloom from one side to the other. There should be two equal lengths of wire, one on each side. Bring these down and twist them round each other to form a stem.

Take care when twisting wires. At first there is a tendency to overdo this. Try to make as few twists as possible. The aim should be to make a unit of two or more wires or of wire and stem. Obviously, if a wire is taken round a stem or round another wire several times with little space between each twist, the result will be a corrugated, thick, ugly 'stem' portion. As a rule, where there are two or more 'legs' of wire, take one and pass it over, round and down the other or others, keeping the space between the twists or spirals as wide as possible. This way the 'stem' will be smoother.

The method of wiring described for begonias can be applied to many other flowers, not necessarily only those with succulent stems, but also for those with very short or almost hidden stems such as hollyhocks, double petunias, stocks, chincherinchees and some kinds of blossom, cherry for example.

124

Wiring bell-shaped flowers

Bell-shaped flowers need slightly different treatment. If they are firm, such as hyacinth 'pips' (the term used for individual florets), they are usually best wired by passing a fine wire, preferably a silver wire although this is not essential, down through the bell from the top. The end of the wire should be made into a tiny loop and as the wire is drawn through the flower this should be allowed to become embedded in the base of the bell. To perfect the wiring, take the wire round the tiny stem under the bloom, two twists are usually enough, and then bring the wire down straight to take the place of a stem.

If a bell-shaped flower is likely to wilt, in which case the corolla will cave in and the bell-shape be lost, first take a piece of cotton wool and mount it like a swab on the end of the wire. Moisten it. Pierce the base of the flower with the wire and gently draw it through until the cotton wool is nestled in the throat of the flower or at the base of the bell, as the case may be.

Some bell-shaped rhododendrons are delightful in bouquets and well deserve to be used more widely. Some of them can be wired in the manner described above, but other varieties fall apart easily after being gathered and these need to be reinforced by crosswires. First insert a lightweight wire up into the base of the flower and then use a crosswire through the base of the bell in the manner described earlier.

Above Lily-of-the-valley needs to be delicately wired. From the pierced top bell the wire should be passed down the stem between the bells. Some people find it most convenient to hold the flower upside down and wire from base to tip.

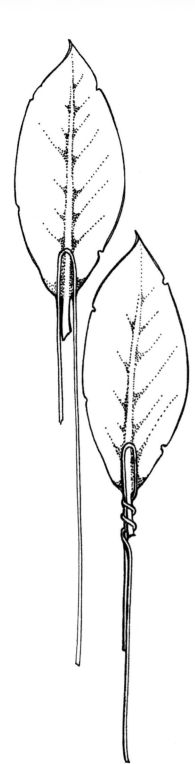

A single-leg mount.

Piercing flower centres

Flowers which have tough, strong centres and hollow stems, such as zinnias, African marigolds, *Chrysanthemum maximum*, helichrysums and many other composites, are very easily wired or mounted. The flower should be pierced from above right through the centre and down into the stem. One end of the wire should be made into a tiny loop and this should become embedded in the centre where it should be quite inconspicuous. It is possible also to insert the wire from below, pushing it up through the hollow stem until it is embedded in the core of the flower. This, incidentally, is a good way of straightening bent hollow stems of any kind.

If after being wired, these flowers appear too stiff, the stem can be bent and the flower 'faced' quite easily.

Mount wires

So far, all the methods of wiring described have involved the insertion of the wire into the bloom at some point or another and although only a few examples have been given, the arranger will find that it is possible to apply these methods not only to many flowers other than those already mentioned, as we shall see, but also to a great number of seedheads and other fruits. However, there is also a method of external wiring which is widely used and which can be applied to a greater number and range of materials, flowers and leaves as well as ribbons and other non-plant items.

Its most important role, I would say, is to mount stems of subjects already wired. For instance, having wired a carnation, it then has to be assembled with others into a bouquet in such a way that it will stay in the position required. It is also important that the handle of the bouquet is formed as assembly progresses. For this purpose, the wired flower is mounted on another wire.

Single-legged mounts

Take a wire and bend one end of it over the index finger to form a loop an inch or so in length. Take the wired flower in the other hand. Lay the loop against the stem, leaving a little of the short end of the loop protruding beyond the base of the stem. Hold the loop firmly in position between finger and thumb. Take the long end of wire and twist it so that it passes twice round the stem, really tightly, taking in the short leg as it goes, then bring it down so that it forms a continuation of the stem.

This is known as a single-legged mount and it can be made with wires of all weights according to the type of flower or other material being used.

Double-legged mounts

There is also a double-legged mount which is used for heavy materials or for those which need to be really firmly anchored. In this case, instead of making a small loop at one end of the wire, the whole wire is bent in the centre, or somewhere near it, so that it becomes hairpin shaped. The top of the loop is placed against a stem in exactly the same way. If you are right-handed, bring the left-hand length of wire over the right and pass it round this wire and the stem two or three times before straightening it and bringing it down parallel with the other leg. Reverse the process, of course, if you are left-handed.

Some unwired flowers mounted by this method result in very dainty work. Take gladioli for example. Individual florets or pips can be used in bouquets, corsages and headdresses. Pull the floret away from the main stem and remove the green-like growth if you wish, although I should point out that by retaining this one often leaves the flowers with a more natural appearance than if it is stripped off. Inspection will show that the gladiolus bloom has a definite back and front. It consists of a triangle of petals within a larger triangle. With the central petal of the outer triangle facing you, place the loop of the mount wire under the flower. Pass the wire round to form a double leg. As you would expect, the lighter and more fragile the flower, the lighter should be the wire.

This is not the only way by which gladioli florets can be wired. Another method is to pass a fine wire through the throat of the floret from back to front and then to bring the two legs down flat against the flower's base and twist one round the other.

Anyone who engages in flowercraft will find these two methods of mounting materials invaluable, not only in floristry proper, but also in everyday flower arrangement. For instance, many kinds of individual dried, preserved and skeletonised leaves used in autumn and winter arrangements have such short stems that left as they are they can be used only low down in arrangements. Mounted and given false stems they can play much more versatile roles. Heavy fruits or bunches of fruit such as tomatoes and grapes can be well supported this way and prove to be much easier to arrange just as you want them.

When mounting wires are used for such purposes, it is up to the arranger to select suitable wires. For instance, a heavy bunch of grapes or an aubergine may need three or more of the thickest wires taken together and used as one. A fragile shadow or skeletonised leaf does not necessarily need a very fine wire if it is to be part of an arrangement. In a bouquet it would need to be as light as possible. If a wire is too fine it will not pass down through or rest upon a stem holder simply because it would bend on contact with any other stem. The stem portion of leaves is usually very

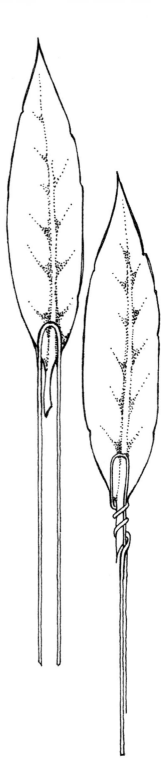

A double-leg mount.

127

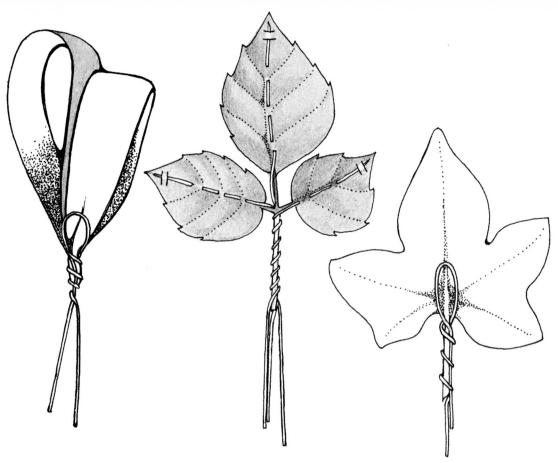

Some of the methods used for wiring leaves.

much tougher than the leaf itself and so will take strong wire.

Often, it is an advantage to use the mount wire in combination with a strong hollow stem or, failing this, with a plastic drinking straw of the right colour. Mount the material and then push the legs of the mount right down inside the stem or straw so that they are hidden and a piece of 'natural' stem remains visible.

In order to take a thick wire any stem can be easily reinforced before it is mounted. Simply lay a short length of wire along the back of the stem. Allow a little to protrude beyond the stem end. Lay the loop of the mount against the wire and the stem. The wire will prevent the mount wire from cutting the stem unduly.

Wiring and mounting leaves

Flowercraft calls for a great use of leaves and so it is necessary to know how to prepare them so that they will retain their beauty until the last. Some are of such a tough texture that it is not necessary to wire them to help them keep their shape or to remain rigid. However, many should be supported by wire in some way, especially if it is feared that they might wilt. This is particularly the case when flowers are to be carried or worn. The obvious thing would seem to be that it would be best to select only those leaves which are of a tough, non-wilting nature, but there are times when other kinds have to be used. For instance, some people like to see real rose leaves used with roses and lilies-of-the-valley with their own forced foliage. One also has to take into account that flowers which are carried are often in surroundings which do not suit them and even tough leaves such as ivy have to be wired because they might wilt.

Some leaves, gardenia is an example, have good, strong midribs. These can be wired by stitching them with fine reel wire. In this case, the wire is threaded through the leaf, near the tip and on each side of the midrib. Thus a tiny stitch is made – and it really should be tiny so that it is almost inconspicuous from the other side. The wire should be carefully drawn through until there is sufficient on the far side to reach round and down to the little leaf stem. Try to make the wire follow the outline of the leaf. You will find that you can guide it and hold it in place with your thumb. Bring the other part of the wire on the other side of the midrib down in the same manner. Twist this round the end of the other portion thus binding it tightly to the leaf stem. From this point you can either trim the wires and mount the wired leaf on another wire or you can leave a length of the leaf wire protruding and use this also as a mount wire. The first method is usually best simply because it is easier to pull the mounted leaf into any position.

Leaves wired in this manner may be curled. In fact, most wired leaves need not look at all rigid and stiff.

Leaves are stitched in ways other than the one just described. Some need to be stitched along the entire length of the midrib or main vein. Palmate leaves may need to be stitched in several places. Here also the stitching needs to be very fine with only a tiny fraction of the wire showing on the upper surface of the leaf. The illustration should show clearly how this is done. As you stitch with one hand, use the finger and thumb of the other to hold the wire firmly in place so that it is not pulled out of place and does not tear the leaf.

Some tiny leaves, such as tradescantia, can be mounted and supported at the same time. Use fine wires and a double leg mount. Lay the loop against the back of the leaf, well above the junction of leaf and stem. Hold one end against the tiny stem and pass the other round both in the manner already described.

In arrangements, some leaves are improved by a little stem wiring, arum leaves and *Begonia rex* leaves, for instance. All that is necessary is to pass a thick or medium wire up through the fleshy stem as far as it will penetrate. Once this is done, the leaf can be easily pulled into position and at an angle it would not have been able to have assumed without this inner support. Incidentally, the same is true of thick fleshy-stemmed flowers.

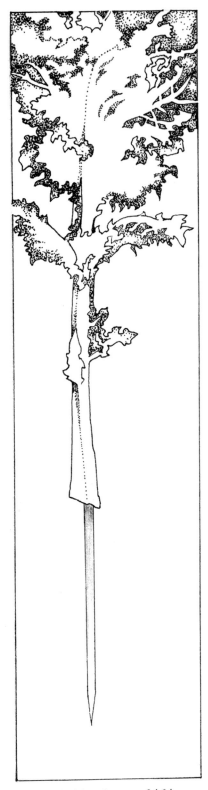

A cocktail stick makes a useful false stem for a large leaf.

129

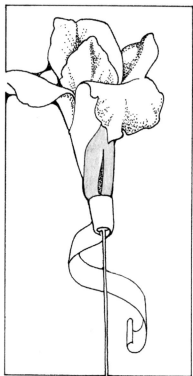

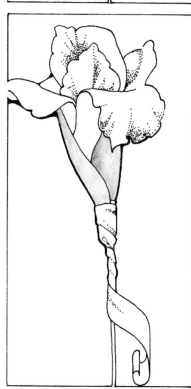

Binding the base of the flower and supporting wire with tape.

Keep a bundle of cocktail sticks with your florist sundries. These make splendid mounts and false stems for several things including large leaves with thick stems. Often handsome and beautiful, these are sometimes much too short to go down inside a container and so cannot reach the water, or the stems may be so short that it is difficult to arrange the leaf to one's satisfaction. I have encountered no difficulty in inserting a cocktail stick in the bases of the short stems.

In some cases, where the leaf soon becomes limp – although if it is first conditioned the danger of this happening should be slight – it is important that the very base of the stem touches the water, but in most cases, the stick itself, which soon becomes damp, conveys sufficient moisture up into the stem tissues. The same thing applies when the materials are arranged in one of the foamed plastic stem holders.

The sticks may be used in the same way for very short, thick-stemmed flowers. They can also be inserted into fruits and vegetables to facilitate their arrangement.

Added support may be given by laying a strip of colourless adhesive tape along the midrib on the underside of the leaf, but the leaf surface must be dry and kept dry. Sometimes a leaf needs several strips laid across its width as well as its length. This method is useful when very large dried leaves are to stand in a hot dry environment. Taping prevents them from curling excessively and thus losing their shape.

There are occasions when certain materials call for slightly different methods of wiring or for the application of more than one method. These will be dealt with specifically as and when we come to them. Meanwhile, we have to learn the method by which we hide the wires and, at the same time, neaten and finish our work.

Hiding wires

This is known as taping or binding. There are many types of florist tape sold for this purpose and I am happy to say that these have gradually improved as time has passed. Tapes may be green, neutral or coloured, usually in pastel tints and white so that they can be harmonised or blended with the materials used. Modern tapes tend to become welded to the wires by the warmth of the hand as one works with them. Wires used for dried materials can be covered with paper. Crepe paper, which is slightly elastic and is available in all colours including a 'stem' green, is best for this purpose. The paper is sold in flattened rolls and tapes are easily made by cutting across the folds.

While florist tape is quite thin, it is not always thin enough to

give a very dainty effect and so, if you find this to be the case, cut it along the centre so that it is halved. I have used a razor blade on the reel to halve the tape, but this tends to weld one layer's edge to another. The best way, although a little fiddling and time consuming, is to ask someone to hold the tape taut while you cut along it with scissors. Incidentally, it is convenient to drape the cut tapes round something so that they can be easily taken up as required. Some people follow a tailor's tape measure method, and drape the tapes round their shoulders.

Taping is better shown than described and I hope that text and illustrations together will suffice to make it possible for you to begin taping right away. Although at first you may be slow and unskilful, I can assure you that this operation, once learned, can be carried out, not only quickly, but also enjoyably.

Begin binding the tape right at the top of the wire, just under a flower or at the junction of leaf and leaf stem, as the case may be. Be sure that the tape is secure and welded before you begin to take it down the stem portion. Really press the tape against the wire at this point and take it right round once or twice so that the end is quite covered. Take the strip of tape in one hand and the material to be wired in the other. If you are right-handed feed the tape with this hand and vice versa. Florists need to become ambidexterous, so as you feed the tape, rotate the portion to be covered. Take the binding down in long spirals. If you make the twists too close to each other the finished cover will look lumpy and clumsy.

When you reach the end of the stem, again make sure that the tape is welded after you cut it. Some tapes are not self-adhesive and in this case it is necessary to apply a little heat to the joins. The best way is to have a lighted candle nearby. Hold the end of the tape above it before applying it to the wire at the beginning and again at the end. Do not put the tape in the heart of the flame or it will become gummy. It is enough to warm it quickly and then to press it well between finger and thumb.

A prayer book bouquet is made on the same lines as one for a corsage. The flowers are backed by a length of the same ribbon used as the book mark for the marriage ceremony. Daintiness and delicacy of work are vitally important. Wired stems should not be twisted around each other in an ugly mass but should be free and part of the general design. Here every wire has been covered with tape. For delicate work this is best narrowed by cutting it down the centre. Once all the materials are prepared, assembly is a matter of a few minutes.

131

Assembling Flowers

Judging by the many letters I receive asking my advice and seeking my help on the subject, there must be hundreds of brides and brides' mothers whose dream it is to make their wedding bouquets as well as to 'do' the flowers. I always point out that this is by no means an easy thing to do without considerable practice and that, certainly, it should never be attempted as a 'once off' job. With practice comes that sureness and skill that transforms a nerve-wracking undertaking into a pleasure that bears with it a wonderful sense of satisfaction and achievement.

Making a corsage

Start modestly and, if you have a goal, well before time. Begin with something that will not take long to assemble, a corsage bouquet for example, and make it for yourself. Having worn it, you will then be able to tell what improvements, if any, are necessary when you assemble the next one. It may, for instance, prove to be unbalanced, with the flower part too heavy or too large in proportion to the stem portion, in which case it will drag on the material to which it is pinned or fail to lie just the way it is required. Practise with all kinds of flowers and, if these are scarce, with any other kind of plant material until you know them so well that you can immediately pick up the correct gauge and wire each one in the correct manner.

A corsage design is one with which it is important to become familiar because it can be applied in so many ways. Basically it is a prayer book bouquet in which the flowers are fixed to a ribbon which also acts as a bookmark. It is also the pattern used to make all kinds of decorative favours such as those already described for gift wraps and for Christmas crackers. More important perhaps to the ambitious, a well-made corsage can form the top and central zone of a bouquet simply by making it of ample proportions. The main difference lies in the angle of flowers to the stem portion. In a bouquet the stem wires are kept parallel to each other – they are later bound together – and bent back from the flowers so that they form the beginning of a handle.

Making a bouquet

In its design and effect a bouquet does not differ a great deal from a flower arrangement and those who can attractively assemble the one should be able to fashion the other. Like a flower arrangement, a bouquet should have a focal point and it should taper at the edges. The fact that all the materials are wired or mounted or both

Above Tying a corsage.

Top right Three ivy leaves are centre stitched for support and the fine wires taken on down their little stems and taped. These three, to save weight, are then mounted on one wire which is then also covered with tape.

is a great advantage in many ways because this makes it possible to arrange the flowers at almost any angle, and often in a much daintier manner than if they had been left on their own stems. I would like to point out that bouquets with the most 'natural' appearance have usually received the most intricate and skilful wiring.

Lightness, both of appearance and weight, is essential and although wires are used to replace heavy stems, it should be borne in mind that wires also are heavy and even these should be kept to a minimum. Wherever possible, mount more than one flower or component on one wire to lessen the weight. As an example, supposing three leaves have to be placed at the base of a flower stem, it may be quite unnecessary to use a mount wire for the flower as well as one for each leaf. It is more than likely that the leaves can be placed against the stem and that all four can be mounted on the one wire.

Where a bud and leaf, the first laid on the other, are to become the tip of a trail or spray, the same applies. When these have been wired and the wire has been brought down round the short stem and beyond it, this wire should be cut short. It will, of course, be covered by the tape. However, there are times when it should be left long; for instance, when it is important that the stem wire of the flower to which the other materials are mounted be really firm. Then all the 'stem' wires can be welded together and taped. Wires should never be twisted round and round each other to make a bulky mass. One fine wire can bind all.

Shapes vary in bouquets and there is really no set rule. They are made from one kind of flower or from a mixture of flowers and plant materials. As in flower arrangement, the first calls for more skill and care than the second if the finished design is not to look too stiff and over formal. Even when it is important that one certain kind of flower be featured it is usually necessary to introduce some other material or materials to provide a contrasting shape. Lilies-of-the-valley are much favoured for this purpose, but almost any kind of spicate flower or flower bud, leaf, or seedhead can be used. Ribbons may also play their part.

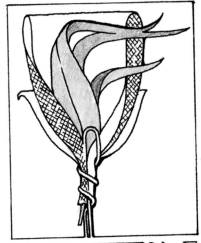

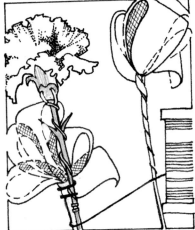

Above and left A posy of carnations with a collar of croton leaves is colour complemented and furbished with loops of spangled net. This is first cut into ribbons. Some loops are bunched in threes or fours.

It is sometimes helpful to make a
bouquet in two or three sections which
are then brought together and bound.
As the lower section is being
assembled, bend the stem wires very
gradually so that later this section will
flow away naturally from the centre.
Have everything wired and mounted
before you begin assembly (*opposite*).
Insert the taped stems in a block of
foamed plastic.

Where one or two kinds of flowers alone are used, these are usually fairly large – for example roses, carnations, begonias, orchids, gerberas – and they are wired and assembled, more or less, one by one as they would be in a vase. They should be so arranged that the design terminates in one of the blooms if the bouquet is small as for a corsage, or there should be one bloom at the tip and one at the base of a large design. Some of these blooms should be recessed, usually in zones round the central flower, so that the finished bouquet has attractive contours. This is much the same as recessing flowers when a bowl of the same kind are arranged for a table. If the sizes vary, the largest, or the biggest mass of flowers should go to the centre and if there is variety in coloration the deepest or the brightest should go at the heart of the design.

When flowers and materials are mixed it is easier, as a rule, to make a large bouquet in more than one section. This way the extremities can be tapered prettily. Sprays of flowers for this purpose are made by first selecting and grading the blooms so that the buds and/or the smallest flowers or florets can be arranged at the end of the spray or sprays.

Obviously, the greater the number of individual components the longer it will take to assemble a bouquet, but I hasten to reassure the reader that it is possible to make a bouquet with just one large, beautiful flower and a little companion material to dress it.

Where the bouquet is to be tapered, the flowers should be graded so that the smallest are at the extremities.

137

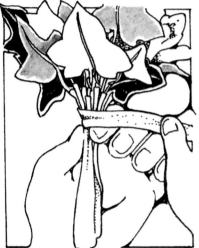

Wiring and binding the handle of a posy. The handle is bent to make it easier to hold.

Posies

The same is true of a posy, which in effect is a round bouquet and stands in relation to the bouquets described above as does an 'all-round' bowl of flowers to a 'facing' vase in flower arrangement.

Posies vary but little, the most popular is the formal so-called Victorian type in which there are well-defined bands of colour round a special central flower. This is usually a rose bud, possibly because this is so well shaped for this purpose. This posy should always be shaped in a slightly conical or dome-shaped manner, like an upturned saucer. It is usually finished by a frill of lace or tulle placed outside a collar of fern or leaves.

The more ancient tussie-mussie is made from a mixture of flowers which is not set in concentric rings round a central flower. It also should be slightly domed and finished with a frill of leaves, not necessarily a collar of material as well.

The loose or informal posy is more a link between the traditional formal posy and a round bouquet. It resembles a little bunch of flowers arranged with their heads together. The stems can be shown, unlike the other posies in which only the flower heads are featured, and tufts of foliage and ribbon loops can be used among the flowers. The posy is set inside a frill which is sometimes made of material which matches the dresses of those who carry the flowers.

Do not make the mistake of making a posy too large. For a Victorian posy, three or four bands of colour are sufficient. Taken beyond this the posy becomes heavy as well as difficult to assemble. Flowers used in this type of posy should be severed from their stems. Parts of flowers and florets may also be used.

The central bloom should always be proud and the circle of flowers should be arranged around it so that they never reach up more than about halfway. Each ring of flowers should be very compact. Bicoloured, tricoloured and multicoloured posies may be made, but the colours should always be in harmony. The hue of each ring should contrast with the one before that of the preceding ring, but it need not necessarily contrast with the one before that. It may match this.

Bouquets and posies need not be confined to weddings. Often flowers to be presented are assembled in one or other of these designs.

Posies can be adapted for many purposes, for certain occasions you can even make several small ones and group them in a garland. A little posy makes an unusual flower arrangement and the stems can be in water in the usual way. Some vases are better than others for this. Once most flowers arranged in the home were posied, and there are still vases made in the shape which was then required with a broad base and a long neck just wide enough to take the

Formal Victorian posies are made in concentric bands of colour or distinct flowers around a choice, central bloom. Here a rose is surrounded by *Viburnum tinus* blossom, then separate hyacinth bells, deep rose pinks and a collar of grey-green senecio leaves. A paper or tulle frill can be added to back this if liked.

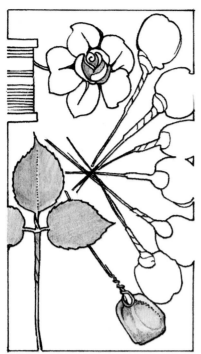

A Carmen rose is made of graduated rose petals mounted on fine wires, bound and taped as a single stem. Any suitable petals, even leaves, can be used in the same way.

stem portion. The posy sits on the top of this. There is no reason why flowers should not be arranged posy-fashion, an easy matter nowadays if the foam plastic stem holders are used. One such arrangement is discussed in the section on Giving Flowers. A tiny posy can be used to decorate and add finish to a gift wrap, or it is possible to make one kind of flower into a posy which resembles one great bloom. A Carmen rose, which also may be worn, is an example of this.

Bouquets for presentation

Generally speaking, presentation bouquets fall into two groups, those which are fairly extensively wired, in which case they are not so very different from wedding bouquets, and those which are left as natural as possible.

In the second case, one should strive to arrange the flowers in such a way that the bunch looks like a specially designed bouquet. It should also be light enough to be carried easily and of such design that it will lie on or across the arm as it is held in the hand. This way it is well displayed. It is usually quite easy to define the way it should be held by arranging a few stems so that they flow down over the stem portion a little way. The stems are important because this type of bunch should be so arranged that it would be possible to stand it in a vase of water where it should look like a flower arrangement. On the other hand, one has also to bear in mind that the recipient may wish to disassemble the bouquet and arrange the flowers in her own way.

One way to protect the flowers and to keep them from being severed from their stems as they are carried around, is to back the bouquet with some attractive foliage against which the flowers can rest. Obviously, a type which grows flat is best for this purpose.

If it is felt that some flowers must be wired, it may be safest to wire them externally so that the wires can be seen and easily removed if disliked. If wires are used internally it is possible that an unsuspecting person might try to snap a stem instead of cutting it and the hidden wire could cause some hurt.

A bunch or bouquet of this type is made in much the same way as a sheaf of flowers, and this in turn is much like making a flower arrangement except that the flowers are held in the hand instead of being inserted into a container.

Lay the flowers on the table or bench in the same way as they are to be arranged, although they should not lie one on the other or they may be difficult to pick up as required. Keep the bunch fairly flat on the table or bench as it grows. Begin with the tallest, central flower, as in an arrangement, and group the other flowers around it, tapering these at the edges, placing the largest in the

Top, left and right, and above Handles of all kinds of bouquets must be comfortable, easy to carry and safe. This is one effective and attractive way of covering the wires.

Left A presentation bouquet once given me by a flower club was simply stood in a suitable vase when I reached home.

central zone, and crossing all the stems at one point. Here they should be tied.

Raffia is a safe tie for this purpose, although a soft green fillis is also frequently used. Do not use reel wire. Avoid twisting the tie round the entire stem portion every time a flower is introduced. Try to make one twist secure more than two stems, otherwise this area will become very bulky. Take care also not to pull the tie so tightly that it damages the stems. On the other hand, these must be firmly secured or the bouquet will not keep its shape. Where a woody-stemmed branch of foliage is used as a backing, this can take the strain as the tie is pulled round the bunch.

It is a pleasant touch to make the focal point of a bouquet of this type from a corsage bouquet which can be easily removed and worn, either at the time or later. After this is made, fasten it to a covered wire which can then be tied in with the other stems.

This is also a good way to introduce small, short-stemmed

A bouquet for our first dear Swiss au pair girl, Ursula. Made from flowers from England, assembled overnight in our hotel room, sprayed and kept cool in the bathroom, here it is in the morning all ready for the bride, but first photographed by my husband Leslie Johns against the handsome curtains.

flowers such as violets or lily-of-the-valley. These can be posied and framed with their own leaves. By keeping them separate this way, it is easy for the recipient to remove them later and arrange them in suitably sized containers.

Cover the tied area with ribbon. Whether extra ribbon loops or bows should be added to any design is a matter of personal taste and I urge that even then they should be used with discretion. There is no doubt that there are times when ribbons can be extremely helpful for increasing the impact of the design or in adding to the colour harmony. Look for water-repellent ribbons in many hues and widths.

Flowers have traditionally been part of May day celebrations in many parts of the northern hemisphere. Here in the lovely Isles of Scilly, where flowers bloom both early and plentifully, children wait with their special May posies for the celebrations to begin. Pyramidal posies like these were also used to top Maypoles around which children and often older people dance.

Headdresses

Like most other floral designs, headdresses are extremely varied. In many cases, all that is required is a form of corsage bouquet which can be worn at one place on the hair, or on each side of the head or of a wedding veil. Of all headdresses, garlands have always been and, one imagines, will always be popular. These can be full, like

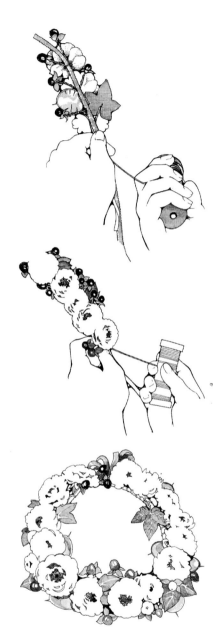

My little 'daisy chain' garland headdress is of pink-tipped chrysanthemums and forget-me-nots backed by grey-green ivy leaves.

Use fine wire and bind the mount wires of the flowers tightly, keeping them on the top surface of the foundation. Bend the garland, arrange the end to match the beginning, secure the two ends and cover the join with ribbon.

coronets, half-circles like tiaras, simple wreaths, either to go right round the head or perhaps small enough to encircle a knot of hair.

I urge any aspiring florist to learn to make a garland with wired flowers and leaves because this is a basic pattern which, time and time again, will prove to be so useful. It can be applied to so many materials and occasions. Ropes of flowers made this way can be applied to special buffet tables. Swags of large and heavy items such as great cones, artichokes, sweet corn, lotus seedheads can be assembled Grinling Gibbons' style to hang on each side of some great doorway. Contrastingly, tiny cones and seedheads can be fashioned into little garlands and used in Christmas decorations. There really is no limit to the application of this design which basically is a rope of flowers protected and backed by leaves. As the rope is assembled the leaves are placed behind the flowers. These not only back the flowers, although they should be barely visible from the front, but also prevent the wires on the flowers from being a nuisance. They might scratch the wearer or they could damage any surface on which they are placed or hung when they are assembled into large, decorative or furnishing designs.

For flowers which are to be worn, very fine wires should be used and where possible these should be covered with tape. Illustrations show how a head garland is assembled. The rope is made and then it is curved. Some people prefer to take a circle of covered

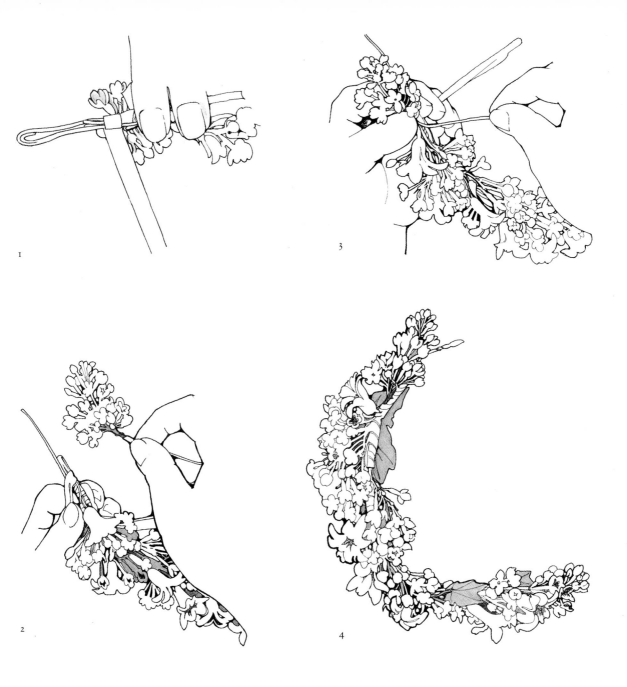

wire as a foundation and to lay the flowers and leaves on this as they are assembled.

It is not essential always to turn the rope into a garland or half-hoop. Simple ropes of flowers are often required. These can be used, for instance, as shoulder straps for a ball dress. They can be fashioned into heart shapes for valentines, into Ms for Mother's Day or for Mothering Sunday. They can also be made as frames, round, oval or rectangular and, for this purpose, dried flowers which last a very long time can be used.

A headdress of lilac and hyacinths with an ivy backing. The individual pieces on fine mount wires covered with narrowed tape are bound together.

To complete the headdress so that both ends look alike, arrange a piece which points in the opposite direction to the others.

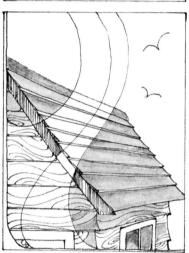

Dried Flowers

Today's dried flower arrangements are to be seen every day of the year. They differ greatly and in many ways from the 'winter bouquets' recommended to readers of women's magazines at the beginning of this century and even earlier. For generations there had been just a few kinds of special flowers, known generally as immortelles and everlastings, which had been highly prized for their long-lasting qualities and for the memory of summer days and flower-filled gardens which seemed to linger in their crisp papery petals. Like the rest of the garden produce they were gathered and stored in late summer and autumn so that they might be enjoyed all winter long. Garden shed doors standing ajar revealed their bunches within, hanging from lines or canes, drying slowly but surely in the cool, airy space. After the first frost they would be taken indoors where they would stay until the fresh flowers bloomed again and homes were spring cleaned and the now dusty flowers were discarded. Then, too, it would be time to sow seed or plant anew for the next winter's decorations.

Those who had flowers to spare carefully bunched them and presented them to those who were especially favoured, but these were bunches in which colour harmony played little or no part. It was the bunches' contents which were of primary importance, and the greater the variety the more they were praised. To go with the flowers, ornamental grasses were cultivated, trembling brizas,

animated oats, fluffy hare's and squirrel tails, stipa, the ephemeral feather grass and others. Those gardeners with glass under their control were able to produce such beauties as Job's tears. All of these served to grace the stiff statice, helichrysums, catananche, helipterums and Spanish clover or gomphrena.

Ladies with time on their hands spent much of it arranging these flowers. Certainly some magazines in gracious prose described ways and means of dealing with the dried stems, but without the modern aids to arrangement which we can employ, these could not have been easy to organise. No wonder that displays were so often squat and always stiff.

Even in the 'twenties the old styles were still in use. I remember so vividly the cottage windows in which bunches of quaking grasses gathered from the downs or fields were stuffed into jam jars, or less frequently into squat vases, to flank a main container filled with the *pièce de résistance*, everlastings of some kind or kinds, which even in the weak and impotent winter sunshine soon became drained of their vital colours. But if you had such treasures you showed them off.

In grander homes parlour mantelpieces looked like little shrines, decorated with tight bunches of the large-flowered statice smothered in a fuzz of one of its smaller-flowered species, or perhaps straw-like helichrysums massed like birds' nests among grasses and yet more statice, all pushed into pretentious vases standing on each side of a matching china clock. Above these on shelves and in alcoves of the overmantel smaller vases held individual posies or even one large individual flower.

In even greater, grander homes there might be also physalis and

statice in baskets in the hall. In some corner of the drawing room bulrushes and tall pampas grasses stood self-consciously in a patterned Chinoiserie vase. Some people actually preserved beech leaves and arranged them on a grand scale, continuing, it was affirmed, a custom begun earlier by none other than Queen Alexandra herself.

These everlastings were all greatly treasured by those who cared for them. Without them, unless one was rich, often there would have been no flowers in the house at all in winter. Gardens had not yet received the wealth of the winter-flowered shrubs they now flaunt; there were not so many cheap cut flowers produced by the commercial grower, or yet the wonderful range of pot plants available to us. But once the houses were better lit and other flowers were available in winter, the long cherished dried flowers suffered a decline.

Dried flowers in modern settings

Nowadays, I am happy to say, dried flowers have come into their own again and are used much more extensively. There are several factors responsible for this, not least of which is central heating. Dried flowers offer a means of decorating a heated interior inexpensively yet very effectively. Better indoor lighting is another important factor. Dried materials need good light to bring them to life. Where they are stood in dim surroundings they simply merge into the background.

Furthermore, in the days when they were used for winter decorations only, everlasting flowers were fairly limited in their variety. Today there are more kinds and varieties cultivated and we know also that it is possible to dry flowers other than the immortelles and everlastings. Because of modern aids it is possible to make dried arrangements for every room in the house, since the colour range is now so much more extensive. It is possible also so to arrange dried flowers that when it is done the decoration much resembles one of fresh flowers. On the other hand, for those who do not want always to conform to set styles in flower arrangement, dried flowers, because they can be mounted and handled differently, offer the imaginative materials from which unusual decorations can be modelled.

Murals

One of my most admired and personally enjoyed flower arrangements in my own home is over my bed. Here most of the wide wall area is framed and filled more than 4 ft (1·25 m) wide, more

148

than 3 ft (1 m) high, with dried and pressed flowers of many kinds. It attractively furnishes the space which lies between the cupboards on each side of the bed in an unusual, pretty, yet practical way. This mural has been in place for years and I freshen it up from time to time when this seems necessary. Besides being a wall decoration my picture is a collection of souvenirs, flowers and leaves with a few seedheads, from friends' plants or from special anniversary gifts, grasses and little pressed wild flowers from some holiday place, leaves picked up in a famous or royal garden, delicate fern fronds from a favourite pot plant. They include many of the true everlasting flowers because I love open-eyed daisies of all kinds, and there are also hydrangea florets, dried delphiniums and larkspurs, roses, alchemilla, pelargoniums, primulas, pressed violets to match the violet-patterned china I collect, and the quaking grasses my young son gathered for me from a local beauty spot.

So many manufactured and expendable items seem far too well designed and fabricated to throw away once used. Many make perfect bases for various forms of montage. Here a talcum box lid holds a spray of dried flowers and seedheads.

149

Montage

I have found that pictures of dried and/or pressed flowers are extremely effective ways of both decorating a wall and adding to the range of furnishings. Colour harmonies abound. There are so many plant materials which can be dried that you can always find something to fit in with any colour scheme, and the muted, natural hues and broken colours have their own particular beauty and will blend with any strong colour you wish.

If you have four attractive matching frames and a bare wall to furnish, you might consider making flower pictures to represent the four seasons. There are leaves, blooms, seedheads and other plant structures which are special to each season and all of which can be dried in some way. Choose a suitable background colour; it may not be good to use the same for each. I always enjoy making winter scenes, fluffy seedheads of clematis and thistle, sprayed with hair lacquer to keep them from disintegrating, look delightful with bare umbels and skeleton leaves arranged around the sturdier forms of white helichrysums, ammobium and pressed woolly leaves of senecio or verbascum.

Opposite A gift for a friend. I knew that she admired maple wood frames, so having found one I set about arranging a bouquet whose subtle flowers would suit their setting.

Below It was my husband's idea that I should 'make one of my flower pictures' in the space over our bed. It changes a little each year, for as some flowers fade or crumble, new ones are substituted, but the general form remains always the same.

One of my favourite 'wooden' decorations made in the style of Grinling Gibbons.

Base materials

All types of bases can be used for plaques and pictures. Many of the everyday expendable objects we handle make surprisingly good foundations for a piece of montage. Cork and other mats of all shapes and sizes and even the large place mats such as those made from split cane or bamboo look really good as wall hangings, and these do not need covering. Such plaques can easily be made into calendars by the addition of tear-off date pads. Even the polystyrene trays in which foods such as mushrooms are sometimes retailed will do. These can be left plain or covered with a piece of material. Rough weave linen looks well under flowers.

Assembling the materials

I usually begin at the centre with the largest flowers and then work my way outwards. It helps if you arrange everything on a sheet of paper first to get an idea of the design you want and of how much material will be needed. I use dried and pressed flowers. The last lie much flatter than the dried kinds and this gives you attractive contours in the arrangement.

Where pressed flowers have stems and also in the case of grasses, fern fronds and long, tapering leaves, I sometimes paint the entire undersurface with adhesive, or put a touch in two or three places, under the thickest part and at both ends. Flowers such as helichrysums need only a touch underneath in the centre. Statice, which is naturally very thick, is best divided into small portions. I hold small things in place with a finger tip for a minute or two to help them adhere. A light weight can be placed on large leaves and on all large subjects when the picture is being assembled on the level. Otherwise one must hold it firmly for a little longer. Obviously quick drying adhesives are best.

When fashioning a bunch or sheaf I make the stem portion from short pieces of dried grass stems. I just dip the thinnest end in the adhesive and push it up under a flower or leaf.

Framing

Pieces of polystyrene can be given frames in many ways. First, of course, make provision for hanging the picture. You can use some of your natural objects to frame the foundation, for instance, overlapping leaves all of one size and kind, a lacy border of tiny umbels, portions of some larger flower. Ribbons, frilled, pinked or scalloped, and gathered net strips also look well in some cases.

Search junk shops and street stalls for picture frames. Many of these are quite cheap and are usually found with old photographs in them. As they are they are not deep enough, for the close-fitting glass would squash the flowers beneath. However, you can easily convert the frame into a box frame by fixing pieces of batten to

Dainty everlasting daisies with grasses. Since I think it is important that in a
sheaf of flowers like this the stems become part of the general design, many
grass stems were saved and arranged to act as flower stems as well.

the back of it. Cut out a piece of strong board the size of the frame
on which to arrange the flowers. You might even be able to use
the original backing unless this is discoloured or shabby. Hardboard used the wrong side uppermost provides a pleasant texture
and a neutral colour as well as a good foundation. Place the box
frame on it, edges level, and pencil along the inside of the battens
to give you the limits inside which you must arrange your materials.
If you plan to use an inner card, paper or ribbon edge apply this
first. Colour or cover the board if necessary. As the flowers are to
be arranged on this you will have to fix the glass firmly inside the
frame. Later, when you come to cover the flowers with the frame,
apply an adhesive around the edges on the other side of the pencil
marks. Fit the batten portion onto the sticky surface. Place a
weight on the frame until the adhesive sets. Make sure that you
have already provided the means to hang the picture.

Making the frame of flowers

Flowers and plant materials which you frame can also be used to make the frame itself. At the time of writing I am relaxing by wreathing an old mirror with soft pink acrocliniums, seedheads and leaves. Perhaps I shall have it done in time to be illustrated here, but in any case it will decorate and enliven a little spare bedroom for which it is intended.

The materials making this frame, like those in the mural, are attached with a colourless adhesive. Usually a mere touch of this is enough, but it is prudent to hold the flower in place with the fingers for a while until you can tell that it has made impact. Leaves are best painted lightly over the entire undersurface or down the midrib.

Some frames, however, I make beforehand and then drape them, or fix them around the object to be framed. I often use what I call my Grinling Gibbons' 'wooden' decorations for this purpose. A favourite ruse is to use them to add distinction to an old mirror, but they look handsome also as wall decorations, hung on each side of a doorway or fireplace. Although I leave mine in their natural state, they can be painted gold or white or whatever is required. Incidentally, I find that these decorations are highly prized as gifts, which indeed they should be, since they involve many hours of work and thought apart from the time spent in collecting the materials used in them.

A ball of non-absorbent plastic foam forms the base for the floral tree.

Right When flowers have strong stems they are easily inserted into dry foamed plastic shapes like these globes. However, helichrysums cannot be arranged this way unless they have been mounted on wires when green as explained in the text. The alternatives are either to glue them all over the shape or to bend a wire and staple them through their centres.

Left Here is the mirror described in the text which was completed in time for photography. The dried flowers, ferns, acorns, gilded hellebores are fixed to the glass with clear adhesive.

Suitable materials

I collect such plant materials as cones, acorns (which should be stuck into their cups as soon as possible or they tumble out once they become a little dry) beech nut cases, poppy seed capsules and seedheads of any kind which appeal to me, chestnuts, conkers, walnuts, teasels, thistles, ash keys, wild clematis, species clematis, dried fennel and parsley umbels, dried hydrangeas, artichoke, lotus seedheads and wild brandy bottles, morning glory seedheads or wooden roses, seed capsules of *Nicandra physaloides*, physalis, and masses of tough leaves for backing, particularly rhododendron species with felty undersides; many, many things so long as they last well and will not quickly become brittle. I also preserve leaves (see page 165) because then they are more supple and I preserve some fluffy seedheads.

Most of the other materials mentioned above need no special preservation techniques or treatment. When necessary I wash muddy cones or any other seedpods such as beech nut cases. These can be dried in a cool oven or simply spread on newspaper and left in a dry, airy place. Clear varnish sprayed on chestnuts and conkers helps to keep these plump, but they have not a long life, nothing like so long, for instance, as walnuts. Those leaves which are not preserved, gathered-up fallen leaves for example, often need sponging and lightly oiling with olive or some other vegetable oil to keep them supple. Rhododendron leaves with a thick, felty underside last best and fortunately these are to be found in several shapes and sizes. The felty portion should not be oiled.

From time to time I blow dust off some of the more ancient decorations by reversing the vacuum cleaner, and after three or four years I take a deep breath, cross my fingers and dunk the whole decoration in a bath of detergent. It is then rinsed under the shower and laid down to drain on sheets of newspaper. So far I have always been successful.

Making a 'rope'

These Grinling Gibbons' pieces are made on the same principle as a rope of flowers described in an earlier section. Usually the components are best mounted individually. Some small items such as little larch cones may be wired separately and then bunched before assembly. Often such a bunch needs some shaping; sometimes it can be posied and surrounded by leaves. I use very small wires for small things and little leaves and thicker wires for others; I seldom, if ever, employ the thickest gauge wires. One has to consider that the number of wires which are involved in making a long rope or swag could amount to a considerable weight if many heavy wires were used.

A backing of leaves finishes the decoration neatly and also makes it much easier to handle and to hang. It is important to have a really good stock of leaves of all kinds before you begin assembling such decorations. Each component, or little bunch or cluster, is backed with a leaf. The toughest leaves should be reserved for the backing. As a rule, since the rope tapers, small leaves should be used at the extremities. I sometimes use pressed leaves in the surface decorations. Small leaves, even foliage tips of certain plants such as the silvery senecio, along with clusters of seedheads and little flowers may be introduced and arranged low down below the larger items.

The wire itself forms the foundation rope in these decorations. The wires are twisted once or twice around each other, very tightly or they will slip off later, at a point just below the piece being mounted, and they are then straightened preparatory to the next leaves and other items being laid below or upon them. As a rule it is not necessary to add a backing leaf each time a surface piece is placed in position. Instead arrange the leaves as they are required, so that when viewed from the back the tips are clearly visible and the leaves overlap rather like fish scales.

Alternatively, you can take a foundation rope and bind the mounted pieces to it. In this case keep the mount wires quite straight and bind tightly.

Just in passing, I should perhaps say that all such decorations need not be 'wooden'. I have made some very pretty ones from dried flowers, with harmonising, prettily tinted seedheads and non-brown leaves, with barley, wheat, oats and other grasses among them.

A rope can be made without a foundation, being gradually built up by the mount wires of the materials used. When these are mixed they should be tapered so that the smallest are used at the ends. Here small larch cones will gradually merge into larger cones. So that they are not too strictly zoned, the rope is gradually made wider by grouping three or four together with other materials between. It is important that the back of a rope should be neat and well covered with leaves.

Wall flowers

Apart from these modelled decorations, arrangements of perpetuelles look well against a wall instead of on a flat surface. If you need a decoration placed higher than usual, you can rest confident that these materials will not quickly fade in the warm higher levels of air. Specially designed wall vases and other suitable containers abound. In some cases you do not even need a vase, for a ball of crumpled large mesh wire netting will do quite well. Hang or fix it in position and simply insert the stems into and through it. Push them in from various angles, including underneath, and you will find that the stems soon lock together and hide the netting. A container or a piece of plastic stem holder placed inside a net, string or plastic bag, can also be hung. Insert stems through the bag into the container.

Where fine stems or a mixture of stem thicknesses are used, foamed plastic stem holder on its own, or a piece inside a wrap of wire netting can be used. Any of these can be hung on a nail or attached to the wall with adhesive clay. If you do not wish to rest the flowers against the wall surface itself, fix the container or stem holder to a backing, a rush mat for example, and suspend this in place.

Arranging dried stems

Because they need not hold water, containers for dried flower arrangements can be as varied as you wish. Indeed, in some cases they need not actually contain the flowers so much as display them. You may, for example, have some attractive figure or little statue which can be used in this way. A ball of wire netting and/or a block of foamed plastic stem holder is usually quite easily fixed in place.

Most of the same rules as those followed for flower arrangement can be applied when using dried materials this way, and these, incidentally, for the sake of convenience are grouped under the umbrella heading of 'perpetuelles'. This covers everything from roots, flowers, seedheads and leaves to fungi.

It often helps to arrange the plastic stem holder slightly differently from when it is used for fresh flowers with water. Instead of filling the vase with it, concentrate on the upper areas and cut it large enough to fit inside the vessel a little way, and also to protrude not only above rim level but in some cases well over it. You will then be able to push some stems in upside down. Containers should be heavy, because the perpetuelles are sure to be light in weight, so if you have to use lightweight vessels fill the lower portion with sand or shingle and place the stem holder above this.

In the style of a tussie-mussie, an arrangement of an assortment of dried flowers, all of which can be grown easily from seed. The pretty downward flow of the little silvery pink rhodanthe is achieved by inserting the frail stem ends upwards into the underside of a dry block of foamed plastic stem holder, which projects beyond the rim of the container for about an inch all round.

158

When stems are wired, hold them by the wired portion so that you put pressure on a reinforced area. Some of the smallest flowers, rhodanthe for example, are best made into small bunches and mounted on one stem wire. If these are to be used as tall stems, arrange the heads at different levels so that you spread the flower portion. Others used at central positions can be posied. Grasses, fern fronds and short lengths of statice stripped from longer stems, small leaves and sprays of foliage, can all be mounted the same way.

Use the largest items at or near the base of an arrangement. Just above the rim or stretching out over it is really the best place for the largest flower heads. Large leaves look well under these rim-level flowers. It is best (and this may be contrary to the way you arrange fresh flowers) to get these in place early in assembly. If you try to push them under other items you may damage them. Arrangements of mixed perpetuelles look best if the materials taper at the edges. This is where you will find grasses, fern fronds, long leaves, or even prefabricated sprays of flowers useful.

Harvesting and drying

Most of the true everlastings dry easily. The bunches should be hung heads downwards in a cool, airy place free from dust, which will dull the colours. Make small bunches and space these out well so that the air can pass all around them. Tie the stems tightly because they will shrink as they dry.

Begin gathering the flowers as soon as they are ready. Daisy types should just be showing their centres, but only just. They will open further when they are properly dried. On the other hand, statice should be well opened or the stems will wilt and the young flowers wither. Condition young stems you might buy by first standing them in one or two inches of hot water, as for beech leaves, page 165. Let them remain in water until properly opened.

Grasses should be gathered young. Too many people wait until autumn to do this when, in fact, they should begin gathering them before haymaking. If you have grown some of the pretty ornamental grasses examine them frequently. The best time to pick them is when the flowering portion is just ready to leave or is freshly emerging from its sheath. Make them into small bunches and dry as you would everlasting flowers. The shadier the place and the more slowly you dry these, the more they will retain their natural colours.

If you want to dry any of the farm cereals, the same rule applies, cut them young.

Bulrushes are really reeds, not rushes. The true grass-like rushes can be treated like grasses. Many people find difficulty in keeping bulrushes, or cat-tails, and complain that they 'burst'. The secret here is to cut them very young. At this time there will be a long bare portion above the velvety flowering part. Cut the stems and avoid touching the flowering part – ever. Remove the top bare tail and arrange them straight away. If you want to store them, keep them in the air for a time until the stems are dry. The bulrushes can then be wrapped and stored.

Always gather all materials on dry days but, if you have no alternative than to gather them wet, swish the bunches back and forth until all the moisture has been thrown off. Strip the leaves from the stems. In hot, dry countries and seasons these will curl and dry quickly, but should there by any moisture in the air they will become mouldy. This mould will spread to the stems and blooms. Examine the flowers from time to time, tightening ties where necessary. Get them indoors before the cold, damp mornings begin if you have them hanging out in a shed or garage.

Most of the everlastings retain their stems and can be arranged on these like any other flower. Strawdaisies or helichrysums, however, tend to drop their heads. The best way to deal with these is to pick the heads only. Spread these out on newspaper or wire netting to dry. They can be provided with false stems in two ways.

The first is done immediately after gathering while the short stem butt, about an inch long, is still soft. Into this insert a 20-g (0·90-mm) florist wire. Push it right up into the flower's centre but keep the end hidden.

To dry these you can bunch the wires and hang them, but they may then become bent. Instead I like to push the wires into some heavy container which will not overbalance. This is either filled with sand or foamed plastic. The wire ends go easily into either of these. Spread the wires out so that each flower is well aired.

The second method gives a more natural look. Use grasses such as Timothy for the stems. Take a thick, strong pin, a slender nail or a cuticle or cocktail stick and pierce the flower's centre from the top. While the pin holds open the aperture push in the end of the grass stem. Pull this through the flower until the base of the flowering part of the grass rests on the flower's centre. Cut the grass level with the flower in such a way that it merges into the eye of the daisy. I assure you that this becomes very easy after a little practice, but if at first you find this method difficult, try this to ease the procedure. Take a short length of florist or fine wire. Push this in immediately after the piercing pin, leaving a wire end projecting up from the flower. Push the hollow end of the grass onto this and then pull the wire right through the flower drawing the grass with it. Remove the wire unless you want it for lengthening the grass stem. Instead of grass you can use 'button' type flowers with tough stems such as those of santolina. I have also seen other compositae centres used, rudbeckia for instance. Much depends

161

Above Among a collection of treen held in an old pottery beaker is a little cone made from all kinds of seedheads, many of them of such a deep texture that the cone itself sometimes seems to be carved from wood.

Right White *Helleborus orientalis* are being made ready for drying in silica gel and Oasis. Outside the box are some purple-spotted hellebores.

upon the size of the flower to be mounted and whether you want the eye of the flower to be dominant or to look as natural as possible.

Flowers other than true everlastings (I have listed them at the end of this chapter) need slightly different treatment. They should be dried as quickly as possible in a warm and dark place. I use an airing cupboard for mine, hooking or tying the stems and bunches over the wooden slats. A cane suspended across the cupboard makes a good line. Individual spikes of delphiniums dry better than bunches. Flat flowers such as zinnias and sunflowers are best arranged so that the flower is flat. A table made of wire netting folded to shape is useful for this purpose. Insert the stems down through the mesh and let the flower rest on the netting.

The same purple hellebores arranged. The stems dried so well that they need no supporting or lengthening wires for this little arrangement.

Drying with desiccants

For centuries flowers have been dried in sand which acts as a desiccant. It suits some things quite well, but it is inclined to press flowers as well as to dry them due to its considerable weight. It is useful for treating flowers for decorations described in the following chapter. The sand should first be dried in the oven and after use it should be re-dried before it is used again.

Much lighter in weight but more expensive are two other desiccants, domestic borax and silica gel, both of which can be bought or ordered from the chemist. You can save a little by mixing sand and borax, one part sand to two parts borax. It is also possible sometimes to buy proprietory drying agents. All of these desiccants can be used many times if they are kept cleaned of debris and dried out again from time to time.

Their advantage is that in them you can dry flowers which would not respond to the methods described earlier. For instance, you can separately dry daffodils, orchids, gladioli. Sometimes I receive a letter asking me if it is possible to preserve a bridal bouquet and this is one way in which this can be done, but it is also a way in which you can discover the shortcomings of the method. If the bouquet is made entirely of the same kind of flower and if the foliage used with the flowers takes just as long to dry, then all is well, but once the materials are mixed it is not possible to make a really good job of the drying because every flower varies in its drying time.

This is why it is no good mixing flowers which are to be dried in desiccants. Each kind of flower should go into a separate container. The drying process is as follows.

Have ready an airtight container. Some of the plastic boxes in which ice-cream is sold are ideal. If you want to keep the flowers on long stems you can use the deep canisters and stand the flowers up in these. However, do remember that the bigger and deeper the box the more desiccant you will need, and this can be quite expensive for a material you will use only comparatively seldom.

The shape and character of the flower give guidance on how to bury it in the desiccant. Faced flowers such as pansies will lie flat, as will some daisies if their stems have been cut off. Pour a little desiccant into the container to cover the bottom. Arrange the flowers on this. They can be quite close but they should not touch. Gently pour the desiccant over them until they are completely buried. Shake the box gently from time to time to ensure that there are no air pockets. Place the lid on tightly and keep it in a warm, dry place.

One way of using much less silica gel is to combine it with one of the dry block absorbent stem holders such as Oasis. Use blocks or slices of blocks to cover the floor of the box. Lay the flowers on this or press their stems into it. Completely cover them with the silica gel, but once they are covered fill the rest of the space with more plastic. I use the crumbled pieces left from flower arrangements, making sure that these are absolutely dry. This saves much silica and hence much expense.

Flowers which are not faced and whose stems are at right angles to their centres should be supported in some way. You can place a layer of dry foamed plastic in the bottom of the box and push the stem ends into this, or you can make a shelf of wire netting which should be wedged inside the container. This is not good for frail flowers because the pressure of the desiccant against the flower and the wire netting often impresses the pattern of the netting on the petals.

Unfortunately it is not possible to say just how long it will take for any flower to become perfectly dry, so much depends not only on the flower itself but on the season. It is worthwhile examining some after 24 hours, but as the flowers may be damaged if you search through the desiccant in order to test them a careful approach is needed. The best way is first to make a plug hole in the bottom of the container or near the bottom in the side and then to insert a cork. When you want to examine the flowers, take out the cork and let the desiccant trickle into a bowl until a flower is exposed. Test it. If it feels papery it is probably dry enough. Flowers left too long in the desiccant will become too brittle.

Flowers which have been cut short before drying need to be mounted on false stems before arrangement. You can save a lot of time by using grass stems and an adhesive. Simply touch the end of the flower's stem with this and apply it to the grass. Sometimes you can push a flower stem down inside a grass.

Preserving foliage

With a stock of preserved leaves you can make your dried arrangements much more varied and natural looking. If you preserve large branches of leaves, keep some of the snippets from the lowest portion of the stems to use in smaller arrangements.

Make a solution of one-third glycerine (buy the cheapest kind) and two parts of boiling water. The stems should be stood in this while it is still hot. However, before you do this make sure that the materials you want to preserve will take water. Some coloured foliage in autumn, for example, may be too near the fall for the stems to be able to operate as they did in summer. So stand everything in 2 to 3 in (5 to 8 cm) of boiling water and leave them in this as it cools until the next morning. By then you will be able to see which branches are worth preserving.

You can begin preserving beech leaves long before the trees turn colour, but the earlier you preserve them the deeper will be the colour of the treated leaves, more like copper beech than

Above A little group of early spring flowers, snowdrops, primroses, pulmonaria, violets, hellebores and crocus, dried in silica gel, displayed in and protected by a glass jar.

Opposite An endearing mixture of dried flowers in a little Victorian vase. The corner in which they stand is often so warm and sunny that fresh cut flowers tend to fade quickly. These perpetuelles are delightful substitutes and suit their setting admirably.

autumn-coloured green beech. There are many other tree and shrub materials which can be treated in this way. Preserve any evergreens at the end of summer when the leaves are tough and mature. Wild clematis or old man's beard seed stems and any of the fluffy garden species can also be preserved and the fluffy styles fixed by using this method.

Some of the evergreen foliage sold by the florist or on market stalls can be preserved to use when flowers are scarce. Eucalyptus, grevillea, box and berberis all respond to this treatment.

Pretty fallen leaves are usually worth pressing. Lay them out between sheets of newspaper and place them under a pile of heavy books or under the carpet. For quick results put the leaves between sheets of tissue paper and press them with a warm iron.

Everlasting value

For really attractive dried flower arrangements there is nothing quite like the true everlastings. Most of these are garden varieties of Australian dried flowers and they are of the daisy family, although not all of them, statice for instance, look like daisies. These are annuals, easy and cheap to grow. Sow the seeds indoors in boxes in February or March and plant them out in the garden after the frosts have finished.

As you can see, this means that they have a short season, for they should be gathered in before the frosts and wet weather of autumn begin.

The kinds of everlastings most grown are *Ammobium alatum*, *A. a. grandiflorum* and their varieties, little white daisies with yellow centres which turn brown; *Helichrysum bracteatum*, straw-flower or strawdaisy (the petals really do resemble straw in texture) which range from white, through yellow, orange, red, crimson, bronze and purple-bronze; Helipterum, the generic name for two flowers usually catalogued as *Acroclinium roseum*, the Australian everlasting or immortelle, sweetly scented daisies in pink or white with double and single flowers, and *Rhodanthe manglesii*, also white or pink with drooping flowers having silvery undersides or calyces and often darkly ringed centres of crimson; Limonium, usually listed as statice, is really a perennial grown as an annual, with colours ranging from blue, violet and rose with white, *L. bonduelli* is a good yellow and there are also apricot and sunset hues in some varieties; *Lonas inodora* has little heads of small, button-like yellow flowers similar to the wild tansy; *Xeranthemum annuum* are dusky pink and mauve daisies which look like tiny shuttlecocks. Finally there is one popular garden perennial, the pearly ever-lasting or *Anaphalis triplinervis*, the white heads of which can be dyed.

Further value

One of the most valuable of all garden flowers, simply because of the shape of the spikes and the colour, both of which contrast so beautifully with the daisies already described, is the delphinium, both the perennial form and the annual varieties or larkspurs, in white, lavender, pink, blues and violet. Others include the tall spikes of *Acanthus mollis* and *A. spinosus* (bear's breeches), which are greenish-purple and white; Achillea or yarrow, of which there are many varieties, and their ferny leaves can also be pressed; *Alchemilla mollis* or lady's mantle, pretty foaming yellow-green flowers; *Angelica archangelica*, great yellow-green umbels; *Catananche caerulea* or Cupid's dart, dusky mauve; *Cynara cardunculus* or cardoon, a giant thistle ideal for outsize arrangements; *Cynara scolymus*, artichoke – those which seem not succulent enough for eating can be dried; Echinops or globe thistle, many species and varieties; *Eryngium maritimum*, sea holly, garden varieties are less prickly and better coloured than the wild species; Helianthus, varieties of sunflowers, the double flowers of which often dry

Byzantine cones are an attractive way of displaying dried plant material. Make some as gifts or Christmas decorations.

well; Liatris, blazing star or button snake root; Solidago or golden rod, all varieties; and *Polygonum bistorta superbum*.

Some of our showy annual flowers dry well. Try *Amaranthus caudatus* and *A. hypochondriacus*, otherwise love-lies-bleeding and prince's feather; *Celosia cristata pyramidalis* or cockscomb is a near relative of the amaranthus and has the same deep crimson chenille look, but also comes in yellow and orange; *Centaurea cyanus* or cornflower, blue and pink; *Didiscus caeruleus*, the lace flower, blue; *Matricaria maritima plenissima* or double mayweed, a pretty little white double daisy; *Nigella damascena* or love-in-a-mist, blue and varied; *Salvia horminum* or clary, purple and magenta, and other salvias including the vivid scarlet bedding variety; and the yellow and light orange coloured zinnias.

I always dry some roses and although these grow dusky with time, they do bring that extra little something to an arrangement. The old-fashioned and rambler varieties dry best, but I have a modern floribunda, Pink Parfait, which I dry every year. I find the flowers which bloom late in the year dry best.

Hydrangeas can be dried but the heads must be mature. The so-called flowers are really bracts and the true flower is a tiny thing in the centre of each. Until this has faded right away the hydrangeas will not dry. Wait until you notice that the bracts are not only turning colour but are changing texture also, becoming tougher and just a little leathery. Let them get tough and well coloured, but cut them before the frosts. These are best hung upside down singly rather than in bunches so that the heads do not get crushed.

Some plants are grown specially for their beautiful seed stems or heads. Among the annuals are *Moluccella laevis*, shell flower or bells of Ireland, which have bright green 'shell' studded stems; Nigella, the seed cases of which are pretty rounded boxes: *Nicandra physaloides*, the shoo-fly plant, with Chinese lantern-like green and black fruits; *Papaver somniferum*, the garden form of the opium poppy which has beautiful blooms and jade green seedheads.

The best known biennial is *Lunaria annua* or honesty, with shiny white satiny seed cases. Teasels are *Dipsacus sylvestris*.

A perennial is *Physalis alkekengi*, the Chinese lantern or winter cherry. The stems of these should be gathered as soon as the first lanterns turn orange.

These are the most important materials. Others are too numerous to list separately but can be classified under headings of grasses, rushes and foliage. However, I should mention specifically pampas grass, simply because so many people ask me how this should be preserved. It needs just the same treatment as the smaller grasses and should be gathered when it first comes out of its sheath. Pampas grass can be arranged right away. Should you wish to keep it until winter, wrap it in paper or polythene and store in a dry place.

Soft grey-green eucalyptus and grevillea foliage with light brown saponaria seedheads frame everlasting daisies, fungi 'lilies', little cones and two light brown 'roses' made from cedar cone scales.

Pressed Flowers

Many of us, on some occasion or another, have opened a strange book and found there, pressed between its pages, some solitary flower, perhaps a primrose, a daisy or a violet, faded maybe but still recognisable, sometimes even with a hint of its original perfume still impregnated in the paper. We wonder who placed it there and why. Was it a souvenir? Did it capture the atmosphere of some wonderful day? Was it the first flower some child gathered or one some lover presented at a first tryst? Was it plucked from a wedding bouquet or brought home from a grave? Perhaps it was none of these things but was placed there casually and simply as a bookmark in the same way that the brewing and cooking herb costmary, Sweet Mary or bible leaf was once used to mark the place in bibles for the church lesson. Whatever its purpose the little flower touches our feelings and we let it remain where it has rested so peacefully and faithfully for so many years.

Not long ago someone gave me a flat green book with the word *Flora* printed on the cover in gilt Victorian lettering. Inside are many pressed flowers and the plain, unprinted pages were obviously intended for this purpose. It is, I imagine, the botanical record of a visit to the Alps since the first group of flowers consists of eight edelweiss and the rest are mountain flowers. Placed between other blank pages there are five more groups of mixed flowers, each group rising up from little pressed cushions of bun moss. They include gentian, mountain viola, soldanella, anemone, delphinium, columbine and others. On the opposite page, which covers and protects them when the book is closed, are their botanical names written in a beautiful copperplate hand.

To me one of the fascinating things is that while I have turned the pages many times not until this moment of writing have I ever studied the flowers from a botanical point of view. Their names are of secondary importance in this case. It is the little flowers them-selves that arrest me and engage my thoughts. Who picked them and when? There is no name, no date on the flyleaf or elsewhere. Where were the mountains and who else was there on those flower-patterned slopes? Were they picked by a young girl, by lovers on honeymoon, a family whose children were learning botany, or perhaps a widow, far from home, seeking to forget her sorrow in some gentle hobby. The flowers reach out over the years, their faded colours, flat silhouettes and papery petals strangely moving. Once more I ask myself, why is it that pressed flowers have this special evocative power? Is this the reason why decorations made from them are so compelling to so many people, for people who press flowers are deeply dedicated as a rule, and is this indefinable appeal also the reason why these flower decorations are so popular with so many people, young and old, male and female alike?

Certainly if you are looking for ideas for a gift, you are almost sure to please if you give pressed flowers. How you use them will depend upon your knowledge of the one to whom you are going to give the flowers. Perhaps most acceptable are flowers mounted as a picture, framed with non-reflective glass and ready to hang. But you can also use them to decorate and/or make paperweights,

A supply of pressed flowers offers an imaginative way of decorating gifts of matchboxes, paperweights, finger plates and similar items.

finger plates for doors, calendars, trinket boxes, lampshades, matchbox covers, book covers, magazine holders, birthday and Christmas cards, bookmarks, and a hundred other things. One of the pleasant facts about the hobby or practice of pressing flowers is that anyone can join in, because you do not need a garden or money to buy flowers. Many of the wayside weeds, buttercups, daisies, clover, hedge parsley, hedgerow leaves, blossom, grasses – to name only a few – will suit your purpose admirably. You can begin even in winter, because there are still frail seedheads and plant skeletons to be gleaned, and then as each small flower takes your eye you can begin making your selection.

Pressing matters

You need very little equipment for pressing flowers, but you do require the quality of patience and a delicacy of touch. If you fear that you may be clumsy, begin with large flowers, leaves and other plant material and gradually work your way down the scale until you can make miniature decorations, even jewellery.

The little book described above is a fine example of patient labour, for it must have taken many hours to press and mount the flowers it contains. Yet pressing flowers is really a very simple operation if you concentrate on simple flowers, but you should allow plenty of time. Even after they have been pressed, mounting them properly takes care, patience and love. Of course, much depends upon how many flowers you intend to press and whether or not you intend to go in for pressed flowers in a big way like two of my neighbours, for whom processing and mounting is a year-long affair. I once met someone who told me that the floor of almost every room in her house was covered with sheets of paper protecting flowers in the process of being pressed by dozens of bricks used to weight them down.

I find that the best way I can fit pressed flowers into my own busy life is to keep a small botanical press constantly filled. This means gathering a few flowers every two weeks or so as they come into season or as I remember them. If I want more, or if I want to press large blooms or leaves, I use a magazine printed on a rough and absorbent paper and lay them between its pages with a piece of blotting paper between the flowers and the print. This is then placed under a pile of heavy books, or sometimes under the cushion of the chair at my desk. This may seem a casual method, but it works. Obviously, if you intend to press many flowers at a time you will need to be better organised.

Blotting paper is best bought in quantity. The same sheets can be used many times, but often one has many in use at the same time, so you need a good supply. Large sheets of blotting and newspaper are needed for full branches of foliage, of field maple for instance, and here I should point out that many pressed materials can be used in dried flower arrangements and similar decorations. I recommend mixing because this provides a greater variety of colours and textures. Hardboard or marble slabs and the sand mentioned in the previous chapter are all aids to good pressing.

For assembly you need stamp tweezers, scissors, fine paint brushes, a skewer, and a knitting needle with a good knob, or with a cork on one end if necessary, so that some of the materials may be held in place while they are being assembled.

It is important to be generous with space when you lay out the flowers for pressing. See that none overlaps another. Keep the kinds separate so that there are not different thicknesses between the same sheets. When you store these, I suggest that you keep them between the pages of a magazine with labels protruding beyond the edges so that you can find them quickly and easily.

Materials should be laid on one sheet of blotting paper and covered by another piece. Spread newspaper under and over these two sheets if you are not placing the blotting paper between the pages of a magazine. They should then be held down and as flat and evenly as possible with the hardboard, marble slab or bricks. Pile more books upon these if the materials to be pressed are thick. Where space is limited, remember that the flowers being pressed can be placed in tiers and in this way will help to press each other. The longer you can leave them before peeking the better, say a fortnight at least.

Even if you are an absolute novice, after a while a few things will become abundantly clear. Some flowers press much more easily than others, many flowers lose their colour and many other flowers change their colours, or reveal tints, shades and tones you had not expected. Thick flowers tend to become bruised.

Choosing flowers

To begin with select simple flowers, that is flowers which seem to be simply constructed, single blooms instead of double-petalled kinds, open faced rather than tubular and with fairly fine petals. As I said earlier, there is so much that you can gather early in the year, and among these materials is the very simply constructed sloe or blackthorn blossom, tiny and delicate, an exercise in patience and accuracy of touch when it comes to pressing. Later you can press more single blossom, plum, almond, apple, pear, wild hawthorn or may.

The buttercup family has many members which will serve you well. The little celandines develop a pure white star at their hearts.

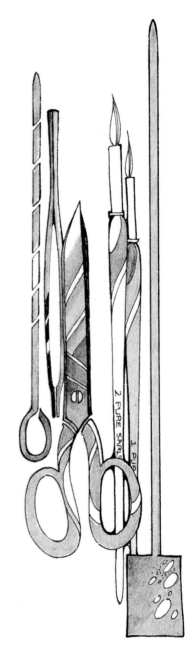

Only simple equipment is needed for assembling pressed flower pictures.

173

Buttercups retain that nail-polish lustre on their petals and their clear butter colour, which incidentally the celandines lose, no doubt because even when fresh they carry much green in their pigments. Lenten roses, the lovely hellebores, will retain their shell pinks and dusky mauves, and the green-flowered species hold their colours well also. Here, though, we meet with one problem: the centres of the hellebores are thick and fleshy and in order to be pressed properly these portions should be nipped or cut out, a practice you have to follow for other flowers with the same characteristics.

Depending upon how thorough you are, or perhaps how much of a purist, you might prefer to reassemble the centre. It really depends upon how flat the surface of the entire group is, for one should bear in mind that the glass which covers the group when it is framed should also press it flat. If there are some components which rise some fractions of an inch above the remainder there may be difficulties. This is one of the things against using pressed nigella or love-in-a-mist, where the lovely seed box is really an essential part of the flower. Personally I prefer to use such flowers in mixtures of dried rather than pressed flowers.

In many cases you can separately dry the thick centre portion of a flower and later slice the top from it and apply this to the flower's centre. This looks better than some alien material.

Still in this same buttercup family, some anemones can be pressed whole, the little windflowers and *apennina* types for instance, but the large poppy anemones, along with ranunculus and paeonies, need to be separated and reassembled as explained below.

Often some tiny flower or calyx can be used to make the centre of such blooms, or these can also be used to make good centres for those blooms such as the hellebores already mentioned which have to have their own thick centres taken away. So much depends upon what flowers you have available or can easily find, but my advice is never to overlook the most humble weed, for it might prove extremely valuable. I once used the tiny seed cases of groundsel in sprays of miniature flowers, and I imagine that one cannot become much more humble than that.

Tubular flowers offer problems sometimes and only rarely do they press well. It is usually best to split them before pressing. Some people cut the tube and press just the wide petal part so that you see the flower full faced as it were.

Primroses and most primulas press well. You will have to decide whether to pull the petal part away from the calyx and then press this alone, or whether to press the entire flower. I find that if you take care it is usually possible to place the flower face down on the blotting paper and then to bend the calyx and stem down so that they lie just between two petals. You can also press the flower

on its side so that it is seen in silhouette. As with most other flowers, I suggest that it is well worthwhile pressing two or three in different ways as test specimens before you launch into pressing a great many of any one kind. Many primulas change colour dramatically after pressing, often with surprising and beautiful results. It is possible to re-group the pressed flowers to make a polyanthus flower. The auriculas are especially good and these will keep the attractive mealy ring at their centres.

Field daisies and some of the larger marguerite types, even the bush daisies such as senecio and olearia press well, as do many of the tiny Michaelmas asters and *amellus* types. Some of the florets from the modern varieties of golden rod can be pressed, although I should point out here that the complete lateral sprays of these

Pressed flower pictures made by a local friend, Joy Strong, who has made this form of flowercraft a speciality with her own particular style. This collection gives some idea of the scope there is in this craft. The tiny picture in the ormolu frame is large in comparison with some of the items she designs, pendants (including the one on the opposite page) and brooches, for example.

175

are most useful for pressing, as they are also, indeed, for drying.

Some people remove the centres, or the greatest part of daisies so that they lie very flat. I prefer not to do this, but I suggest that you experiment and make your own decision. Often the backs of these flowers are very attractive, with pretty overlapping scales on the calyx.

The pink-tipped buds of the field daisies should be used with the open flowers. If you think these are too thick, carefully slice them in half. The thick centre can then be taken out before the half buds are pressed.

Do not overlook buds in general, because although we need the more vivid colours of the wide-open flowers, we also need the contrasting shapes and the family association of their buds. Without them there is often a sameness about the assembled flower groups. Certain buds, especially those in sprays, can also provide a graceful shape to place at the edges of an arrangement. I especially like the bud sprays of larkspur and delphinium which, although pressed, I sometimes use in dried flower arrangements, as well as the soft silvery buds of the bushy senecio which I think is among the most loveliest of all perpetuelles.

But to return to the daisy family, among which are many flowers with an abundance of petals. These may be pulled apart if you hope to use them. Personally I do not really see the point of disassembling a chrysanthemum to have to put the petals together again in your own way, when you can use a complete multi-petalled flower such as a helichrysum, but this is a matter of personal taste and it depends also upon the nature of the decoration. African marigolds, which keep their colour well, are much too thick to press, but their individual petals are worth treating. From these you can make attractive wide-eyed flowers, if you wish with smaller daisy types as their centres. Where the grouped petals make a fairly thick flower, whole dried buttons from cotton lavender, or santolina, or tansy can be used instead.

Sometimes the many-petalled flower can be kept entire in a sense. It can, for instance, be halved, by which I mean that a substantial number of the centre petals should be removed before the flower is pressed. Turning to my Victorian book mentioned above, I see that there are many thick flowers there (though not multi-petalled flowers of course since these are species) and none of these have been pulled apart. If dry silver or horticultural sand is used to press thick flowers instead of the paper sheet method, these can be kept entire. When they are mounted, bear in mind that flowers of the same thickness should be grouped together.

Another way to deal with thick flowers is to dry them first in desiccant to remove most of their moisture before pressing them. Two or three days should be sufficient for most kinds. Flowers dried this way usually keep their stamens and centres whole

Daisy-type flowers make good subjects for pressing but they may need to be cut in half first to reduce the bulk.

although they are likely to shrink somewhat during the process.

I always have some fern fronds of some kind under the press, mainly because it is so easy when one walks in the garden or in the fields or lanes to pick one or two fronds and it takes only a few minutes to strip off the side frondlets, or, as in the case of maidenhair fern, to separate the sprays and to place them between paper. I have one acquaintance who presses the latter fern to use as cake decoration with icing sugar and crystallised flowers.

Pressing leaves

Leaves are essential in arrangements and some press very well. Usually the finer their texture and the more patterned the surface the more attractive they look after pressing, but remember that some leaves can be pressed for dried arrangements. These can be thicker and tougher and can sometimes be pressed on their branches; it is necessary to experiment a little. Perhaps because I have had such success with fern, I tend to press leaves of a similar appearance, such as hedge parsley, chervil, Sweet Cicely, dicentra, lacy maples, rue, thalictrum, tree lupin, as well as compound leaves such as robinia and some of the rose species. If the last two are pressed when they are young they will not separate after pressing but if you find that this does happen, spray the compound leaf with hair lacquer before using it. The compound leaves of wild vetch are very dainty and some species have little tendrils as well. The nearly related clovers also are attractive, especially if you search for those kinds which have good leaf markings.

I press quantities of the foliage of woolly and so-called silver plants and these are used in dried arrangements as well as in pressed flower decorations. If you have them to spare, whole rosettes of the downy verbascum can be pressed in dry sand and later used as focal points in large arrangements. Leaf skeletons or those of other parts of a plant are as attractive in decorations made from pressed flowers as they are in dried flower arrangements and montage.

Leaf skeletons

Often one can find natural skeletons of leaves and all that is necessary as a rule is that these should be washed so that they are free of mud and dross, then dried and pressed. If you wish to make your own skeleton leaves, select only tough-textured kinds such as pear, magnolia, laurel, lime, camellia, oak, and any kinds you find which appear to become skeletonised naturally. Crowd these into a vessel filled with rain water. The leaves should be immersed. Let the water stand out of doors in the sun for several weeks, topping up the water level when required. As it is essential that

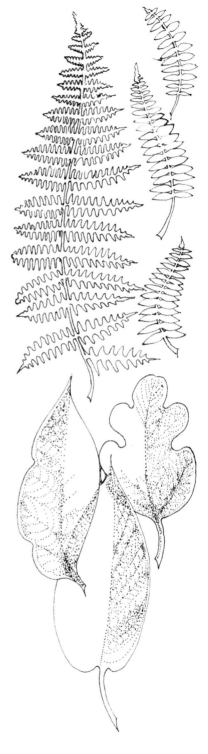

177

I like to keep a small flower press
constantly filled, gathering the flowers
every two weeks or so.

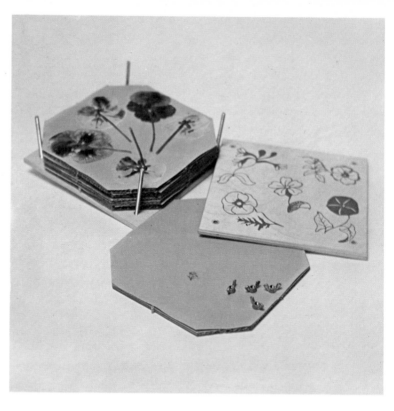

there should be bacterial activity in the water, it will become smelly
and slimy and very discoloured and unpleasant but do not change
it. After a few weeks test a leaf or two to see if the fleshy upper and
under sides have rotted. Rub a leaf very gently between finger and
thumb. Eventually it should become slippery and the outer tissues
colourless and at this point it should be possible to pull away the
outer surfaces. I usually speed this operation by using a large
darning needle, which I insert near the midrib at the stem end. If
the leaf is ready I can easily lift the layers and peel them away from
the tissue skeleton. This should be done gently.

The skeleton or shadow leaf should then be washed under a tap
until all traces of green tissue are washed away, a matter of a few
moments. If the leaves are dingy they can be made brighter by
soaking them in water to which domestic bleach has been added.
Dry them by laying them as flat as they will go on newspaper
before pressing them.

In my opinion these plant skeletons are invaluable to those who
intend making pictures of pressed flowers. It is important to
realise that although many flowers may be brightly coloured when
they are first assembled, their colours do fade in time. However,
their shapes and textures are usually so lovely that they remain
beautiful and continue to give pleasure. It is for this reason that
unless you are featuring just one kind of flower, you should seek
to vary the materials as much as possible. The skeletons offer de-

lightful contrasts of texture and they can be grouped with thick matt flowers so that one enhances the other.

Some flowers and some seedheads will skeletonise well but their preparation often calls for time and patience. You may find naturally skeletonised cases of the ornamental physalis around the faded plant, but if you grow the edible kind you can skeletonise the cases quite easily and quickly. Poppy heads and most other fibrous seed cases such as Canterbury bells, hollyhocks, moluccella, nipplewort and campion can be treated as described above.

Cards decorated with pressed flowers and foliage have many uses beyond the obvious means of sending birthday or Christmas greetings. For instance, when you send a flower arrangement which needs special care, perhaps to be topped up with water daily, use the card to give details. If it is pretty I am sure that it will be kept long after the flowers have faded. This Mother's Day arrangement, incidentally, is in water-soaked foamed plastic stem holder in a plastic tray used for retailing food, covered with a doily in the same manner as that used for the Easter egg arrangements.

The importance of stems

When stems are featured in pressed flower groups and pictures they should be treated seriously. Often a picture is spoiled by the application of, say, merely three stems, when a mass of flowers has been grouped together. Save the finest stems of grass for this purpose. Keep a look out for suitable material which can be used as a main stem for any flower sprays you may assemble. Often stems of climbing plants are good for this. The wild white bryony, for instance, is very fine and also has really curly tendrils and tiny leaves and flowers. Young stems often press better than the tougher, more mature growth. Broom branches, often prettily curving, are also worth pressing.

Greetings cards and tags are a useful starting point for decorating gifts with pressed flowers.

Display

You may wish to do no more than to reflect in your pictures and decorations of pressed flowers your attitude to all flowers and to flower arrangement generally, in which case you will display them as naturally as you can. In grouping them you simply follow the main rules of flower arrangement: large flowers to be placed low and central, tapering materials to go to the edges, all to appear to be springing from one unseen central point. You can follow the lessons already learnt about colour harmony and contrasts of shapes and forms as well as proportions. The latter applies especially if you arrange the pressed flowers in a 'container' made perhaps from plant material, maybe even from another pressed flower, or maybe from a shell. Proportion is important, too, in framing; a group should suit its frame. My own preference is for this natural representation and it is this aspect which is featured in this book. However, I should point out that some people enjoy using pressed flowers and other materials as though they were paints or collage materials. From them they make pictures which are not arrangements of flowers so much as representational land-scapes, still life, even portraits of birds and animals as well as abstract designs of great diversity. The same methods of pressing and mounting apply to these.

If pictures made of pressed or dried flowers are to look effective and be truly decorative they should be well mounted and framed. You cannot be too punctilious about this, and if you have doubts I suggest that you begin with some lesser items, there are many from which you can choose. It is important to realise right at the beginning that pressed flowers are very frail and must be handled delicately if they are to remain fresh and undamaged, so my advice is, first become familiar with them. Get used to handling them. To begin with leave aside all thought of covering them with tricky transparent surfaces. Concentrate instead on learning how to group them most attractively. Once you are pleased with your pictures, then it will be the time to display them in such a way that they will last for years.

When a young acquaintance of mine, anxious to use pressed flowers, asked me what she could make first of all, I suggested Christmas cards. I thought that this would appeal to someone who had little pocket money to spend on commercial cards and I knew that she was interested in and enjoyed her art lessons at school. I thought that once she became proficient she was likely to make some very pretty cards indeed, and this proved to be the case. All kinds of cards, Valentine, Easter and birthday, as well as gift labels, menus and place name cards are good things to begin with. Individually, cards do not need many flowers, a good point if you are just beginning and do not have a large stock of materials. Each one of these cards will not take so long to assemble, which means that you can soon apply lessons learned to the next item you make. In decorating these cards you will discover how important it is that surfaces should be kept clean, edges cut really straight and that a professional finish is really half the secret of success.

If you haven't a separate workroom with a table where you can leave your materials undisturbed until you next have time to take them up again, try to keep everything on a tray so that nothing need be moved.

It helps considerably first to make a rough design of how you want to see your flowers grouped. You can simply spread them out on a piece of paper, but you might find it more helpful if you have a matching piece of card or paper. This way you can tell precisely how far into the centre or out to the edges you can place one thing or another. Obviously the test card can be no more than a piece of paper of the correct size.

I search junk shops and stalls for old photograph and picture frames and often I find that I can use most of the mounting material still under the glass. Otherwise the flowers can be mounted on photographic mounts or good stiff card.

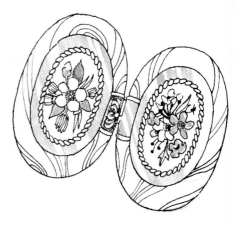

A tiny pressed flower picture occupies each half of this locket.

Assembly

How you apply the flowers depends very much upon the design. The notes given for dried flower pictures earlier apply to pressed flowers in most respects. I use a latex-type adhesive for most things. Usually all one needs is the merest touch of this; too much of it and it will not only show but it will raise the flower from the mount. Bear in mind that the adhesive is simply there to keep the flower in place, the glass will hold the entire group.

One drawback arises when the flowers are to be covered with a self-adhesive transparent cover such as Fablon. This can be tricky, and when large groups are to be covered the flowers tend to be lifted out of place as the material passes over them. In this case it is helpful to paint the adhesive over the entire undersurface of each component part of the design so that it will remain firmly and safely in position. Thick materials, tough leaves for example, or halved seed capsules which might be used as 'containers' in pressed flower arrangements, need more adhesive and for these the clear, quick-drying types appear to be best.

When you arrange tiny petals and flowers for the first time you might well believe that your fingers are all thumbs. As a rule it is not easy to lift and place the petals without the aid of some tool or another. I have a slim, pointed paper knife with which I lift the frailest materials. I use tweezers for those I know are not likely to bruise or crack.

The adhesive should be applied to the base of the underside of the leaf or petal with a skewer, knitting needle or very fine oil paint brush. Lift the petal onto the blade of the knife, quickly turn it and taking it to the group lower it into position. Use the side of the knife to edge the object into place if it doesn't fall quite as you want it. Then take a small piece of blotting paper and with your two fingers pressing on this hold the object in place for a moment or two.

Whole flowers should have the adhesive placed in the centre of their underside. When holding these in place press the knob of the knitting needle or cork into their centres and hold it there for a minute or two. Alternatively, place a cork in position and weight it down.

Straight stems often need only one touch of adhesive, at the point where they are to appear to flow from the group, but if they are curved they may need more. Dot the adhesive at intervals following the parts most curved. Press down with the blotting paper or place a weight on the paper for a few minutes.

How you arrange the flowers is up to you. A first reaction is usually to place them into a sheaf-like group, but as in all other forms of floristry, informal patterns need not be faithfully followed. You could, for instance, place the flowers in a Victorian posy pattern; in concentric circles around one central bloom and finish off with a collar of leaves. If you have several flowers of roughly the same size they can be arranged like an informal posy or tussie-mussie. There is no reason why you should not add a little paper frill. If you are at a loss for ideas, use a kaleidoscope, mirroring some of the flowers, petals and leaves you would like to use.

Pressed flowers are ideal for book-marks. I made this one on a strip of strong paper covered by gauze to strengthen it and to add texture. The flowers were then glued to it, lightly pressed again and then covered with transparent adhesive plastic sheeting. The ends were fringed with scraps of gold-edged ribbon. Small roses and blossom with full centres and thick-petalled flowers such as these hyacinths are often best dried in a desiccant before pressing.

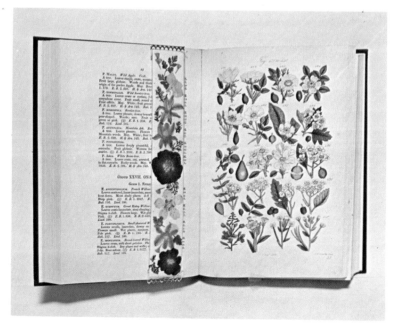

Pressed flower decorations

The kind of decoration you use for cards can be applied to book-markers, box covers and little trinkets of all kinds. Bear in mind that pressed flowers on objects which are likely to be handled can become damaged and it is for this reason that they should be covered. If you have some way of neatly and inconspicuously securing its edges, plain transparent plastic film can be used for this purpose, but it must be well stretched and uncreased if it is to look well. The self-adhesive coverings are good once you have mastered them. I suggest that you make a few practice runs with unimportant flowers so that you find the snags.

More simple objects which will take pressed flowers are candles, and even the domestic white kind can be transformed in this way. It is quite safe to light the candles when they have been decorated. Add fragments of scented plants such as lavender leaves, rosemary flowers to give off a slight incense or perfume as they burn.

There are many ways in which candles can be decorated apart from simply fixing the flowers in a random pattern over the surface. One can wreath the candle at the base, taking the flowers at least

Just a few of the many varied pressed flower decorated items made by my neighbour Sheila Coates. She uses simple materials so attractively and in fascinating patterns, not only garden flowers but such wayside plants as daisies, buttercups, clover, May blossom, silverweed foliage and hog-weed seeds among many others. Her gifts include calendars, outsize match boxes, doorplates, pictures and paper-weights. The little candle is mine.

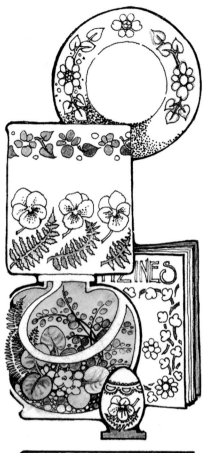

a quarter of the way up and making a pattern of the tips. One can make a 'rope' to twist around the candle from base to tip. Rings of flowers, of separate kinds possibly, can be passed around the candle at intervals.

As you would expect, many small flowers are suitable for this purpose. I would suggest that instead of painting the individual tiny flowers with adhesive, you paint a band on the candle itself. Make this narrower than the width of the flowers for it will spread when you apply them, and apply it very lightly. Lay the candle down as you work. Get all the flowers in place, then hold them down lightly to ensure that they are anchored.

Another technique that requires some practice and skill is to make use of the candle wax itself to hold the flowers in place. Holding the candle by the wick, dip it in hot water for a few seconds to melt or soften the outer surface. This surface will then accept and hold the plant material. After considerable practice it is possible to lay out the decorative material in such a manner that the warm candle can be rolled gently over it to hold it on the surface.

Egg shells, whole blown kinds or used breakfast eggs, can also be prettily decorated with pressed flowers. These can be applied individually in bands of kinds and colours, or in a random patchwork over the entire surface. If you fear that the shells may be too frail, they can be filled first with paraffin wax. An entirely covered shell can be lacquered. Use a colourless spray lacquer and apply it lightly.

While I have been writing this my thoughts have been racing off on pressing campaigns of their own and once my desk work is done I hope to try some of the ideas which have been coming into my mind. They include a lampshade with pressed houseplant leaves to go on to a carboy in which little houseplants are growing and which for a long time now I have been intending to turn into a table lamp. There are also a tray and a table top, both of which can be covered with adhesive transparent film. Then there is a white china plate to use as a wall decoration. Flowers may have to be lacquered to this and it will require a little experimenting. My magazine folders and book covers can be covered with strong plastic. No doubt once I begin more ideas will come. I am sure that the imaginative reader will also think of more. If you are resourceful into the bargain you may think also of easier and quicker ways of applying and protecting the flowers.

Meanwhile, I hope that some of the items illustrated will suggest to you ways and means of using your own pressed flowers right away. I hope also that they support a remark I made at the beginning of this chapter, that anyone can take part in pressed flower decorations because such simple plant materials can be used and given a new beauty as well as a different role to play.

List of Common and Botanical Names

African Marigold – *Tagetes erecta*
Allspice – *Pimenta officinalis*
Animated Oat – *Avena sterilis*
Arum Lily – *Zantedeschia aethiopica*
Balm – Melissa
Bay – *Laurus nobilis*
Bear's Breeches – Acanthus
Beech – Fagus
Bells of Ireland – *Moluccella laevis*
Bergamot – *Monarda didyma*
Bible Leaf – *Chrysanthemum balsamita*
Birch – Betula
Blackthorn – *Prunus spinosa*
Blazing Star – Liatris
Bluebell – *Endymion non-scriptus*
Borage – *Borago officinalis*
Box – Buxus
Bracken – *Pteridium aquilinum*
Brandy Bottle – *Nuphar lutea*
Broom – Cytisus
Bryony – *Bryonia dioica*
Bulrush – *Scirpus lacustris*
Burnet – Sanguisorba
Buttercup – Ranunculus
Button Snake Root – Liatris
Campion – Lychnis
Canterbury Bell – *Campanula medium*
Caraway – *Carum carvi*
Cardoon – *Cynara cardunculus*
Celandine – *Ranunculus ficaria*
Chamomile – Anthemis
Chervil – *Anthriscus cerefolium*
Chinese Lantern – *Physalis alkekengi*
Chives – *Allium schoenoprasum*
Christmas Rose – *Helleborus niger*
Clary – *Salvia sclarea* or *S. horminum*
Clove – *Eugenia aromatica*
Clove Gilly-flower – *Dianthus caryophyllus*
Clover – Trifolium
Cockscomb – Celosia
Columbine – Aquilegia
Coltsfoot – *Tussilago farfara*
Coriander – *Coriandrum sativum*
Cornflower – *Centaurea cyanus*
Costmary – *Chrysanthemum balsamita*
Cuckoo Flower – *Cardamine pratensis*
Dandelion – *Taraxacum officinale*
Double Mayweed – *Matricaria maritima plenissima*
Elder – Sambucus
Feather Grass – Pennisetum
Fennel – Foeniculum
Gay Feather – Liatris

Gilly-flower – Dianthus
Globe Artichoke – *Cynara scolymus*
Globe Thistle – Echinops
Golden Rod – Solidago
Gorse – *Ulex europaeus*
Groundsel – *Senecio vulgaris*
Hare's Tail Grass – Lagurus
Hawthorn – *Crataegus monogyna*
Heartsease – *Viola tricolor*
Hedge Parsley – Torilis
Hellebore – Helleborus
Holly – Ilex
Hollyhock – Althaea
Honesty – *Lunaria annua*
Honeysuckle – Lonicera
Hops – *Humulus lupulus*
Hyacinth – Hyacinthus
Hyssop – *Hyssopus officinalis*
Indian Corn – *Zea mays*
Ivy – *Hedera helix*
Jamaica Pepper – *Pimenta officinalis*
Jasmine – Jasminum
Job's Tears – *Coix lacryma-jobi*
Jonquil – *Narcissus jonquilla*
Lace Flower – *Trachymene caerulea*
Lady's Mantle – *Alchemilla mollis*
Larkspur – Delphinium
Laurel – *Prunus laurocerasus*
Lavender – Lavendula
Leek – *Allium porrum*
Lemon-scented Geranium – *Pelargonium crispum*
Lemon Thyme – *Thymus citriodorus*
Lemon Verbena – *Lippia citriodora*
Lenten Rose – *Helleborus orientalis*
Lily – Lilium
Lily-of-the-Valley – Convallaria
Lime – Tilia
Lotus – Nelumbo
Love-in-a-mist – *Nigella damascena*
Love-lies-bleeding – *Amaranthus caudatus*
Maple – Acer
Marigold, African – *Tagetes erecta*
Marigold, Pot – *Calendula officinalis*
Marjoram – *Origanum vulgare*
Marrow – Cucurbita
Meadowsweet – Filipendula
Mint – Mentha
Mint, Variegated Pineapple – *Mentha piperita citrata*
Mock Orange – Philadelphus
Moon Daisy – *Chrysanthemum leucanthemum*

Mullein – Verbascum
Musk – Mimulus
Myrtle – Myrtus
Nasturtium – *Tropaeolum majus*
Nipplewort – *Lapsana communis*
Onion – Allium cepa
Opium Poppy – *Papaver somniferum*
Orris – *Iris germanica florentina*
Ox-eye Daisy – *Chrysanthemum leucanthemum*
Paeony – Paeonia
Pampas Grass – Cortaderia
Pansy – Viola
Pine – Pinus
Pineapple – Ananas
Pinks – Dianthus
Poinsettia – *Euphorbia pulcherrima*
Poppy – Papaver
Primrose – *Primula vulgaris*
Prince's Feather – *Amaranthus hypochondriacus*
Privet – *Ligustrum ovalifolium*
Pumpkin – Cucurbita
Pussy Willow – Salix
Rhubarb – *Rheum rhaponticum*
Rose Geranium – *Pelargonium graveolens*
Rosemary – Rosmarinus
Rue – Ruta
Sage – *Salvia officinalis*
Sandalwood – Santalum
Sea Holly – *Eryngium maritimum*
Shell Flower – *Moluccella laevis*
Shoo-fly Plant – *Nicandra physaloides*
Sloe – *Prunus spinosa*
Smilax – *Asparagus sprengeri*
Snowdrop – Galanthus
Southernwood – *Artemisia abrotanum*
Spruce – Picea
Squash – Cucurbita
Stocks – Matthiola
Strawdaisy – Helichrysum
Sunflower – Helianthus
Sweet Cicely – *Myrrhis ordorata*
Sweet Corn – *Zea mays*
Sweet William – *Dianthus barbatus*
Tansy – *Tanacetum vulgare*
Teasel – *Dipsacus sylvestris*
Thyme – Thymus
Tree Lupin – *Lupinus arboreus*
Variegated Pineapple Mint – *Mentha piperita citrata*
Vetch – *Vicia sativa*
Violet – Viola
Wallflower – Cheiranthus
Watercress – *Rorippa nasturtium-aquaticum*
Winter Cherry – *Physalis alkekengi*
Woodruff – *Asperula odorata*
Yarrow – *Achillea millefolium*
Yew – Taxus

Index